LETTERS TO HOME

Letters to Home

A MEMOIR
(& OTHER STORIES BY AN ABC)

JANETTE WU

NEW DEGREE PRESS

LETTERS TO HOME

A Memoir (& Other Stories by an ABC)

ISBN	978-1-63730-608-6	*Hardcover*
	978-1-63676-920-2	*Paperback*
	978-1-63676-984-4	*Kindle Ebook*
	978-1-63730-088-6	*Ebook*

Thank you Mom and Dad for letting me air-dry my dirty laundry on the clothesline and not disowning me for it. I love you both even if neither one of us will admit it.

Table of Contents

Read This Before Reading Anything Else

A Letter to My Readers

Dear Readers,

If I'm going to be honest, writing a book wasn't at the top of my bucket list.

There was a greater chance that I would go skydiving than convince myself to write a book. Instead of jumping out a plane with a 170-pound man backpack strapped to me, I chose to dive into the void of an empty page—both of which evoke fear and diaper-wetting, respectively.

But since you are most likely leaning against a bookshelf perusing hundreds of memoirs or Asian American authors, then you know one of those things has been checked off the list.

There is an adage that says life will always find a way to throw you a couple of curve balls—even if you've spent your entire life being that one kid in the corner of the gym dodging them.

There are three main reasons that I decided to begin this book journey rather than chase that adrenaline rush at 14,000 feet.

1. I am ~~uncomfortable~~ comfortable sharing information about my experiences.
2. The COVID-19 pandemic
3. Memoir writing = legacy writing

COMFORTABLE WITH BEING UNCOMFORTABLE

My friends always tell me I keep too many secrets—that I don't "tell them anything" or I don't "talk about myself much."

In response, I would say, "Ask me anything; I'm an open book."

But that is a fat lie, and I know my friends know it too.

In reality, secrets and privacy are things I hold very close to me. I've grown up in a traditional Chinese immigrant household so early on, I learned how to hide report cards—or what the prep school calls "progress reports"—even before I knew that there was a designated word for my actions. The only progress I was willing to share was a grade, anything above 100 percent.

But even outside of the instances where I "lost" my exam paper by turkey-stuffing it into the abyss of my backpack, secrets and privacies were second nature to me. It always felt unnatural and even unsettling for me to "release" information about myself in conversations. Oversharing information about myself to others made me feel uncomfortable, even if it was not brag-worthy information.

Therefore, one of my goals for writing this book is to combat this insecurity—to willingly air out my dirty laundry and put myself in uncomfortable situations. Because it is only when we get comfortable being in uncomfortable situations that we can experience the most growth. Or, in the words of Brené Brown, in her 2018 book *Dare to Lead*, *Letters to Home* is my attempt at "rumbling with vulnerability."

Hence, at its core, this book contains some of my secrets and memories stored in separate time capsules. Each time capsule contains a collection of letters and essays, dedicated to my family, and now, to you. These letters and essays detail my upbringing in NYC as an American Born Chinese (ABC) woman diving into the intersections between Chinese-American culture, heritage, identity, and all the feelings suppressed and shoved underneath the rug in a traditional Chinese household.

In the first capsule, *Read This to Cure Homesickness,* I dive into how my Chinese immigrant parents chose to express love as well as certain Chinese traditions common in my household.

In the second capsule, *Read This to Embark on a New Journey*, I uncover one of the

"D" words forbidden in my household while taking you through the beginning of a lifelong journey of (re)learning Chinese, a language I am already supposed to know.

In the third capsule, *Read This to Hear My Inner Thoughts,* I give you a glimpse of what keeps me up at night. I will share thoughts about my identity, my upbringing in the city that never sleeps, and my experience traveling back to my parents' hometown in rural China.

In the fourth capsule, *Read This for a Dose of Nostalgia*, we will travel back in time to experience my version of summer vacations circa 2009 along with what it is like to grow up with a younger brother.

In the fifth capsule, *Read This for a Moment of Reflection*, I share my thoughts on our inevitable reality surrounding death and the grieving process.

In the sixth capsule, *Read This to Teleport to the Other Side of the World*, I take you to my motherland and share what it is like to be an ABC in Mainland China and the "leveling up" of my language learning journey.

Lastly, in the seventh capsule, *Read This When You Have Read Everything Else*, you will find two final letters from myself and my dad.

For my fellow friends who are also ABCs or children of immigrant families, I hope these stories resonate with you. While some of these anecdotes are common in the Asian American diasporic experience, others are solely unique to my upbringing. Although this memoir is not representative of all ABCs, I still hope to create a sense of belonging in these shared experiences. As we all continue to connect the dots of our past to present, I hope this book can leave you with an ounce of inspiration to share your story too. There is enough space on the bookshelf for all of us.

THE COVID-19 PANDEMIC

When shit hit the fan in March 2020, I was forced to quarantine in my childhood home becoming roommates with these "time capsule feelings."

At the height of this outbreak, death was (and still is) unforgiving and all around us—creeping around every corner and hiding behind every shadow. After my capstone year in China was abruptly cut short in February 2020, I sat myself down and read Paul Kalanithi's 2016 book *When Breath Becomes Air.*

The memoir is about a neurosurgeon who, when faced with a cancer diagnosis, attempts to grapple with the meaning of life and death—a question he spent his entire life trying to answer. Frankly, this book took my breath away (no pun intended). It redefined my perception of this simple yet convoluted concept: death.

Since finishing Kalanithi's book, this taboo topic of death keeps resurfacing and making its unwanted appearance—forcing itself in the form of two questions:

1. Do we only seem to notice things (like death) when and only when we are constantly reminded of its existence?
2. If yes, why should we have to wait until death is knocking on the front doors to finally knock down the bastion of our hearts to be open and express how we really feel to our loved ones?

When Breath Becomes Air remains one of my main sources of inspiration behind this book. Kalanithi's book, my past experiences, and the 2020 pandemic have taught me that everything can be traced back to two things: Life is fragile, and tomorrow is never guaranteed.

I recognize that even at twenty-two years old, I am living on borrowed time. I am too young to think I am running out of time but also too old to believe I am invincible to the many inevitable realities that come with the journey of life. I am also not too optimistic to assume that I will always have "tomorrow" to express my love and appreciation to those around me.

After reading this, it is right to assume that death is the recurring theme in the upcoming pages of this book. But I am here to debunk that myth. As much as I would love to channel my inner sixth grade emo girl, this book takes a (mostly) lighthearted and humorous stance on otherwise heavier topics.

All this depressing shit about life and death was a driving force for me to write this book. The thought of an invisible timer ticking in the background was enough for me to conquer the negative thoughts and questions about whether I was qualified enough, old enough, or mentally strong enough.

This was a heavy reminder that if I don't tell my story now, then when will I? And more importantly, *who* is able to tell my story better than I can? This uninviting, overbearing gray cloud of death hovered over me for most of this pandemic. Yet this cloud also acted as a source of motivation that pushed me forward to write another chapter and control the narrative around my story.

LEGACY WRITING

In the beginning of this book journey, I came across the phrase *legacy writing*, a term used to describe the memoir genre. On the surface, this book is a mere collection of letters and stories about a twenty-two-year-old ABC (American Born Chinese) woman and her upbringing in New York City. But I realized that below the tip of the iceberg, this memoir has the potential to be an artifact providing evidence of family lineage stories for my future descendants. As a result, this book is also my attempt to build a bridge between my past ancestors and my future descendants while simultaneously breaking down cultural and language barriers.

As a first-generation child of a Chinese immigrant family, I was forced to learn how to navigate international waters while in my country of origin. While growing up under the influence and privilege in New York City, everything became about survival of the fittest. I felt that if I wasn't constantly proving to others that I could be the smartest, fastest, strongest, and brightest crayon in the box, I was at risk of being exiled for not being "American enough."

When I was younger, I thought that somehow, my accomplishments would grant me access to the exclusive American club. As a result, I became an overqualified and underpaid hamster on a wheel, constantly chasing the next "big thing" to prove my worth in exchange for a badge of belonging.

But now, being American enough means I can own up to the individuality of my upbringing without being apologetic. From the conflicting Chinese versus American values to transgenerational cultural and language barriers, I've curated a repertoire of some of these thoughts and experiences here in this book.

In addition, this book is a constant self-reminder to be fearless in the pursuit of my truth. By diving deeper and exploring the topics and experiences written in between the lines of Asian American culture and heritage, I hope to normalize the conversation around traditionally taboo topics like death, identity, and cultural barriers. By having these conversations, we can make more guided decisions in our lives; confronting and reevaluating our day-to-day routines and conversations to make sure they align with our core values. In doing so, we can bring these topics to light, even if it makes us feel uncomfortable or uneasy.

I hope some of these raw and personal anecdotes can resonate with you, whether you are a fellow ABC, Asian American, a child of immigrants, or simply someone who likes to read memoirs like Michelle Obama's *Becoming* or Ali Wong's *Dear Girls*. Consider this a bootleg version of your favorite memoir, a fresh and entertaining perspective of a twenty-two-year-old ABC who isn't going to lie to you that she has life already figured out.

Nonetheless, I am humbled you are here reading the words I have spilled on the page as a form of distraction amid the 2020 pandemic and post-undergrad life crisis. Thank you for allowing me to share a small piece of my life with you. I hope this book prompts self-reflection within our own relationships with our family, friends, and most importantly, ourselves.

From the author and your favorite ABC girl next door,
Janette

TIME CAPSULE I

Read This to Cure Homesickness

CHAPTER 1

A Bowl of Fruit with a Side Piece of BBQ Pork

Dear Mom and Dad,

I could write an entire book for all the things I am appreciative of, but at least in this chapter, I want to thank you both for choosing to raise me instead of raising a piece of pork. I understand there were many pros and cons to both decisions, but I am glad you both decided I was a better investment.

Dad, do you remember when you always told me and Derek about how you started cooking for your siblings when you were just five years old? At five years old, I didn't even have the strength to pick up our non-stick pan, so I question the logic of that story.

Regardless of all the times we complained, "Ugh, not bitter melon again!" or "There is too much ginger, green onions, and oil!" I feel fortunate to have savored every Cantonese dish you whipped up in our kitchen. I hope you know that despite the both of us being twenty-something, the best

Derek and I can do is chicken fried rice and pasta. If it isn't obvious already, we are better at eating than cooking.

In the following pages, I reminisce about the times actions spoke louder than words. There's that famous saying in American English: A picture can mean a thousand words. In Chinese it is, "书意能达万言." In this case, a bowl of fruit can mean a thousand "I love you's." If that's the case, then I can only wish I can send a basket of fruit back home every day.

From your daughter who is always willing to eat but never willing to wash dishes,

Janette

WHEN I'M ASKING FOR A FRIEND

My mom once threw the dirty pan in the sink and said,

"生你有咩用? 生旧叉烧好过生你!"—"Why did we even give birth to you? We would be better off giving birth to a piece of *char siu* (barbecued pork) instead of you!"

Disappointed Chinese mothers use this sarcastic Cantonese saying whenever they scold their children for misbehaving. Hence, in the Wu household, my mom used this to let me know I was a good-for-nothing child who wasn't helpful with the chores around the house.

I am no economist, but I'm about 87 percent sure it is cheaper to raise a piece of pork than to raise a kid. And as for another added bonus, a piece of pork won't talk back to its parents like I did.

This saying is merely friendly banter. My mom and grandma weren't serious about wrapping me up in tinfoil, taking me to the local butcher, and exchanging me for a juicy piece of pork. On second thought, what is the social services number again?—I'm asking for a friend.

After ten minutes of taking the hard blows from being compared to a piece of pork to being asked "点解你唔可以乖啲?"—"Why can't you just be a well-behaved child?"—I dragged myself off the couch and dutifully washed the dishes like the obedient, well-behaved piece of pork I was raised to be.

WHEN DINNER IS READY

One weekend during my sophomore year of college, I charged through the stairwell door of my grandparents' first floor after a long commute back home. The first floor always had the lingering aroma of whatever my grandma was cooking on the stove, along with the scent of burning incense and old people pajamas.

Grandpa was sitting in his usual spot at the dining room table. His swollen legs were already propped up on the leg stool, and he was routinely shifting through the tray of orange pill bottles filled with medications. A couple feet away, Grandma was hovering over some pot on the overworked stovetop with an oil sifter in one hand and an empty bowl in another. I grabbed a handful of chopsticks and put it to the side of the twenty-year-old table still covered in the original plastic wrapping.

I couldn't help but snap a quick picture of the food that my grandma was cooking in the wok and sent it over to my boyfriend, Rauful. The meat was glistening under the range vent hood lights and nicely marinating in the simmering sauce. I was drooling more than Pavlov's dogs. (Spector, 2014)

I sent the picture over to my boyfriend, Rauful, and said, "Dinner is ready! I'm starving."

He replied, "Wow! That looks delicious. What dish is that?"

My thumbs twiddled over the keyboard on the screen, trying to think of the name of the dish.

"Braised chicken..." *Backspace.* "Braised beef..." *Backspace again.* "Braised meat...I think."

I tapped on my grandma's shoulder as she was transferring the dish from the wok to a clean plate.

"嫲嫲，依个係咩餸啊?"—"Hey grandma, what dish is this?"

She said some name of a dish I don't recall.

"咩肉来嘅?"—"I mean, what kind of meat is this?"

"猪肉" —"Pork," she replied.

"哦，咁依个呢？"—"Oh, what about that one?" I said as I pointed to another dish on the table.

"猪肉"—"Pork," she said.

"依度入面嘅係咩来嘅?"—"What's in here?" I said, gesturing to the big pot still simmering on the stove.

"汤...."—"Soup..."

I let out a sigh. "Oh thank God..."

"猪骨汤"—"Pork bone soup."

I stared at her in disbelief and then asked if there were any dishes that weren't pork.

She gave me a dumbfounded look that revealed her thought of why she didn't turn me into a dinner dish for asking such a stupid question.

She pointed to the dinner table again and said, "依碟梗係鱼来嘅啦!"—"Of course! There is fish!"

Afterward, I hesitantly texted back, "Pork...everything is pork."

Did I mention my boyfriend is Muslim?

As a devout Muslim, Rauful can only eat halal meat. Pre-Rauful, my uncultured ass had no idea what the term "halal" meant besides the fact that he can't eat pork. It is only after meeting him that I found out that "Halal" is an Arabic word meaning "lawful" or "permitted." In Chinese, "halal" translates to 清真, which means "purity" and "cleanliness."

According to the Islamic Council of Victoria, the Islamic law on slaughtering animals is designed to minimize the pain and suffering of the animals. This procedure is done by a trained specialist who uses a surgically sharp knife in one swift motion. The name of God is also said in order to emphasize the sanctity of life and that the animal is being killed for food with God's consent.

The opposite of "halal" is "haram," which means unlawful or prohibited. Halal and haram are universal terms that apply to all facets of life, commonly used in relation to food products, meat products, cosmetics, personal care products, etc.

To all Muslims, eating pork is haram. But depending on one's interpretation of the religion, some would eat animal-based protein, like chicken, beef, and duck, while others would only eat halal meat—that is, chicken, beef, and duck, or another animal-based protein prepared with the minimal suffering procedure.

Growing up as a Gen Zer, I learned to love turtles, hate straws, and give a shit about the effects of climate change. I also watched my fair share of documentaries that made me want to go vegan because of the mistreatment of animals.

This is why eating halal meat seems like the perfect compromise, one that takes a more humane approach for our omnivorous selves. But as an individual who also tries to be environmentally conscious, I found myself at a crossroads between choosing my culture's tradition of eating pork and my value of doing the least harm on our planet Earth. Things get even more complicated when immigrant parents use cooking as an expression of love.

After learning about Rauful's dietary preference, I didn't think it was a big issue. In fact, it helped narrow the planning and coordination surrounding the dreaded couple question, "What do you want to eat?" However, I didn't realize this was a bigger issue for my parents—but that's a story for later on.

WHEN THE APPLE DOESN'T FALL FAR FROM THE TREE

When I wasn't savoring my grandma's food on the weekends, I spent most of my week reheating leftover takeout food at the dorms. One night, during my sophomore year in college, I was hanging out in the eighth-floor lounge, taking my second forty-five-minute break of the night. It was mid-November 2017, right after midterms and a few weeks before finals week. As expected, instead of getting a head start for final preparations, I was procrastinating.

My friend Sophia had sent over *The Five Love Languages* quiz, a personality quiz that gives insight into how people express and receive love differently within five different categories: acts of service, words of affirmation, receiving gifts, quality time, and physical touch. This quiz applies to all relationships—especially married or dating couples—but it also applies to our relationship with our parents. After taking this quiz, I wondered what my parents' love languages were and whether their love languages have influenced me.

When I was growing up, I would watch a lot of American TV shows and Disney Channel movies. The teenage daughter would leave the house and the parent would say, "Love you—have a great day at school!" and the daughter would nonchalantly reply, "Love you too—bye!" as she swipes a piece of toast from the breakfast table.

Scenes like this often stuck out to me for two reasons. The first is that these American parents have enough time in the morning to make breakfast, plate it nicely on the table, sit down, and enjoy their breakfast with their morning paper and cup of Joe. In comparison, during weekday mornings, my Chinese parents were rushing me and my younger brother out the door with a Tupperware of Frosted Flakes cereal to eat on the car ride to school.

Before I transferred elementary schools, the car ride to school was at least forty minutes (thank you, NYC morning traffic). During the car ride, my brother and I would unconsciously raise our Tupperware bowl of cereal milk in the air whenever we are near the highway bump. We learned our lesson the first time we thought we could *ride out the wave* but that only resulted in a chest full of soggy flakes. On some days, breakfast would be the high-fructose-corn-syrup-injected cereal. On other days, there would be a sad hotdog dipped in cold ketchup. Nonetheless, both days were served in a plastic Tupperware—never on a ceramic plate with accompanying toast, sunny side eggs, or crispy bacon.

The second thing that struck out to me was how foreign the movie's dialogue was to my reality. The *L word* is never spoken out loud—at least in my Chinese household. Whenever I witness scenes like this in movies, something always feels out of place. My family did not speak or express their love verbally; instead, they expressed it through actions.

Afterward, I realized I wasn't being fair to my parents for their inability to express love how traditional white Americans do without considering my immigrant parents' childhood environments. When my parents were growing up in the villages of Taishan, China, they lived in drastically different times. They considered meat a luxury (which helps in explaining why they are *obsessed* with pork now), but more importantly, their families' main focus was survival.

My parents learned to express love from the way their parents expressed love, which at the time consisted of bringing home food and the occasional meat product. Hence, it is only logical that my parents grew up thinking that love should be expressed and reciprocated through these acts of service and gift giving.

That is why for them, "I love you" is replaced with "Have you eaten yet? I'll make you some food."

"How are you? I hope you are doing okay," is replaced with, "I made you a bowl of fruit."

However, for me, nothing screams "I love you" more than having someone's undivided attention during deep talks at 2 a.m. Perhaps this is a sign that I am shifting away from a materialistic mindset and becoming, dare I say, more aware of the little things in life. Nothing is more personal and intimate than sitting in the presence of your loved ones or simply helping me fold the laundry when I am swamped.

I've come to realize the form of love I crave cannot always be fulfilled by others. Especially when I have immigrant parents who work full-time to keep a roof over my head. I am forced to look inward and give myself with the quality time I crave.

When I retook *The Five Love Languages* quiz for the second time, my results were 37 percent quality time, 27 percent acts of service, 23 percent words of affirmation, 13 percent physical touch, and a shocking zero percent for receiving gifts. When I first took the test, my top two love languages were also quality time and acts of service. However, I don't remember getting a fat zero for receiving gifts. Don't get me wrong, I love gifts. Even more so, I love the intention that goes into buying the perfect gift. To my friends and family, please don't use this as an excuse for showing up empty-handed at my next birthday party.

This quiz led me to reflect on how I ultimately express love. Although my love language is zero percent for receiving gifts, I paradoxically express my love in this exact manner. It turns out that my way of expressing love is parallel to how my parents do so through acts of service and gift giving. The apple doesn't fall far from the tree, does it?

WHEN GIVEN BITE-SIZED LOVE

There are many instances in my life where I would coop myself up in my room. During middle school, I would catch up with the friends on ooVoo (the Zoom video communication platform of 2009) even though I had just seen them a few hours earlier. Then throughout high school, I would pull all-nighters, passively reading the same paragraph of a textbook for the third time.

Sometimes, my parents could hear bursts of laughter. Other times, they could hear quiet groans of frustrations and stress from the heavy school workload. However, to my parents on the other side of the locked door, it all looks the same.

They would often call my name from the other side of the house.

"JUNE-NET!" my grandma would scream from the floor beneath me.

"咩"—"What is it?" I would scream back.

Silence.

"咩"—"What is it?" I screamed again, more frustrated this time.

Silence.

That is when I would drag myself out of my room and put out whatever fire my grandma needed extinguished on the first floor of the house—which usually required me to unplug, then re-plug the TV cable.

Other times, my temper would get the best of me, and my patience in the danger zone. Then I would snap back at my parents faster than a turtle with a finger dangled in front of him.

There was a time during my junior year of high school when I was knee-deep studying for three Advanced Placement (AP) courses.

"Junior year is the most important year!" said everyone from the college counselors to the neighbor's cat.

"I know. I heard it the first twenty-seven times you said it," I would mumble to myself.

I was rereading the same paragraph in my AP United States History (APUSH) textbook when I heard an abrupt knock on my door.

Knock knock.

The sound of the knock took me by surprise and I screamed out, "咩"—"What is it?"

Knock...knock.

I rolled my eyes and immediately felt an incoming wave of frustration. I dragged my feet toward the bedroom door and just before I even opened it, I screamed, "WHAT IS IT? WHAT DO YOU WANT?"

My mom stood a foot away from me with a wide smile on her face, impervious to my burst of anger. My face softened and the waves of anger immediately retreated. She stood at the doorway, holding a small bowl of fruit in her hands. I looked down and saw the couple of wedges of apples and a handful of strawberries staring back at me.

She said with a big grin on her face, "食生果"—"Here, eat some fruit!"

I quickly grabbed the bowl and slammed the door. My body immediately surrendered to the overwhelming emotions as I sat back down at my desk and stared at the bowl of fruit as it now sat in my hands. My vision blurred from the tears when the wedge of apple I picked up between my fingers came into focus.

On the surface, it was just a bowl of fruit—a snack for my hours spent on writing APUSH outlines. But what wasn't visible in this bowl were the hours that my parents spend going to the supermarket, picking out the best fruits, carrying them home, sometimes even surviving a few bumps in the car ride, washing them to be free of dirt, peeling them to get rid of the stubborn pesticides, carefully cutting them into bite-size wedges, and finally plating them into a bowl to deliver to my doorstep. They displayed their ways of offering condolence through immense acts of service—the same acts of service I hope to one day attempt to reciprocate.

And as I drowned in an endless stream of tears and snot, the tears rolled down my face into the bowl and ricocheted into my APUSH outlines. The blue ink bled from one sentence to another, but in that moment, the deadlines and assignments seemed insignificant. That night, with an apple wedge in one hand and a blue pen in another, I thanked the universe for my parents, their ways of expressing love, the homemade Chinese food, clean water, a roof over my head, and finally, my parents' decision to raise me instead of a piece of pork.

CHAPTER 2

A Taste of Home

Dear Grandma,

Do you remember that one afternoon in April 2021 when we took the bus home together after your doctor's appointment? When we got off the bus by the corner deli, you tapped on my shoulder and whispered, "我好想食牛油Bay-gull。你要同我一齐食吗? 我次次都想食, 就係唔知道点讲。"—"I'm really craving a bagel with butter. Do you want to split one? I always want one, but I never know how to say it."

I immediately laughed and smiled at the innocence of your question. I was surprised that you could still eat bagels even with your dentures. But truthfully, I was even more surprised that you showed interest in a food apart from the Asian food that you normally cook and eat.

Over the years, you spoiled my taste buds with your Cantonese home-cooked meals. Sometimes I wonder if instead of eating your sweet and sour pork, I would be eating Chef Boyardee canned spaghetti and meatballs for dinner. When I cooked in the dorms, I tried my best to replicate your famous dishes. A sprinkle of this, a splash of that. Somehow, your definition of "少少" —"a little bit" of soy sauce is always different from mine. Since then, I have a greater appreciation for you and the time, effort, and love that you pour into cooking our family meals.

I don't say this enough but thank you for your countless sacrifices and words of encouragement. I can't imagine what it's like to start a new life in a foreign country with a language that you don't speak and a culture that you aren't familiar with. Yet despite all the financial, cultural, and linguistic challenges, you still persisted. It makes me wonder if you would even need my help to buy a bagel if we were still living in mainland China.

Nevertheless, it makes me happy to know I can help bridge the gap between you and my American world of toasted bread with holes in the middle. This small act of service is microscopic compared to all the years you spent taking care of me. Through your occasional "back in my day" lectures, I was able to remain grounded—to find a footing in the Chinese culture that no history book or history channel can ever teach me—for me to say I feel fortunate would be an understatement.

By the way, remember to show the deli guys the Post-it note I wrote for you in case I am not home when your cravings kick in.

With love from your granddaughter who also loves toasted cinnamon raisin bagels with butter,

Janette

WHEN IT WAS BACK IN MY DAY

It's easy to spot my grandma in public.

She's that old Chinese lady sitting quietly on the D train, unaware her cell phone has been ringing for the past three and a half minutes. All the subway riders, including the train conductor himself, could stare at my grandma, but she is too busy thinking about the soup she is going to make that night. It's most likely one of those twelve-hour soups that require a black chicken from a butcher hidden in some alleyway. It also isn't a twelve-hour soup unless it is mixed with some dried herbs that some auntie smuggled into the states twenty-five years ago.

As I was growing up, I would go downstairs and find my grandma with her head hovering over a gigantic soup pot. I'm sure that if it's possible, she would hook me and my brother up with IV bags filled with her renowned soups. Each drip would serve as a constant reminder to not waste her hard work.

"This is good for your skin," she would say as she pats my right cheek.

"This will make you pretty!" she would say as she pats my left cheek.

Most of the soups were warm and comforting. Others were purgative at first sniff, with one bowl strong enough to flush out the toxins faster than those five-day kale juice cleanses.

Every other night, she would hand me a bowl. And every other night, I would give her the same look I give others when they tell me they bite their fingernails.

"好贵噶! 你一定要饮晒佢。汤冻咗就唔好饮噶啦，趁热饮。"—"It's very expensive, you must drink it. It's not good when the soup is cold, drink it when it's hot." My grandma would say in response to the disgusted look on my face.

"但係, 个汤好苦啊!"—"But, it's so bitter..." I would reply.

"你咪埋眼, 一口气就饮晒啦！我煲咗十二个钟噶!"—"You can just close your eyes and drink it in one gulp. I spent twelve hours making this!" she persisted.

Over the years, I learned to stop asking questions about what was in my grandma's soups. This is because she would mistake my curiosity for a second round of more soup.

I would hold the bowl up to my face, allowing my lips to rest on the rim of the bowl. The seemingly never-ending abyss at the bottom of the bowl stared back at me, and I thought to myself, *The quicker I drink it, the faster I can get rid of the taste of potentially endangered species brewing in my mouth.*

I gulped it down.

Even from a young age, I understood the dire consequences. If I refuse to drink it, I am signing up to listen to a fifty-minute lecture on "Ungratefulness: Why You Are Lucky to Have Food and Soup on the Table?" I've been to this lecture enough times and know they all begin with, "You know, back in my day..."

Back in her day, New York City wasn't the way it is today. When she immigrated to the states in the late 1980s with my grandpa, my dad, and his siblings, the city was run by the crack epidemic and the trains were covered with graffiti. With a language barrier and only an elementary school diploma in hand, she did what she knew how to do to survive: She worked at a textile factory in the Lower East Side of Manhattan.

"I was one of the fastest sewists in the factory!" she would say in between bites of food.

During these rare occasions when I sat down and ate dinner with her, I could not help but admire her perseverance and tenacity. It took ten years for her and our family to save up to buy a house in Brooklyn. To others, it may have just been another place to live, but to my grandma, it was a home in a foreign country—a home bought by the hard-earned pennies and hours on hours of hard work.

As I was growing up, she wasn't able to help me figure out negative numbers or geometry proofs, but she did what she knew what to do. She filled our bellies with food and soup... so many bowls of soup.

WHEN PATIENCE IS A VIRTUE

As I was growing up, my grandma and parents would cook mainly Cantonese style dishes. My family is from Guangdong, a province in the southeast region of mainland China. Hence, most of my meals at home were Cantonese seafood and rice dishes, which included steamed fish, clay pot rice, sweet and sour ribs, and stir-fried string beans that my grandma grew in bulk size in the backyard.

The flavor of these dishes is what Chinese people would call 清淡 or on the "mild side" of the spice spectrum—and by mild, I mean, the spice is virtually nonexistent. Cantonese-style food strives to bring out the freshness of the original ingredients rather than drowning it out with spices and sauces. These dishes were lightly seasoned and sweet in taste, but strong in flavor. Besides picking out the ginger and green onions, I practically inhaled every dish that came out of the kitchen—without ever questioning the source and its origin.

Until my first year of learning Chinese in college, I had wrongfully assumed the Cantonese dishes I ate at home were the standardized norm in China. This was because Cantonese style dishes were the only "Chinese-style" dishes that I was exposed to. I knew that Chinese food was more than just the General Tso's chicken takeout (which is just an Americanized version of *real* Chinese food). But I didn't realize how the twenty-three provinces in mainland China have incredibly different styles of cooking and food. In reality, there are the delicious seafood dishes from Shandong province (Northeast China) and the infamous throat-numbing spices in the Sichuan province (Southwest China).

Before learning all this, I had no idea there were *eight* different cuisines—I also had no idea China wasn't just one big province. When I signed up for the Chinese major during my freshman year of college, I didn't realize the importance of learning Chinese beyond the surface level. I was surprised that even after growing up with the culture for those first eighteen years, there is still so much I have yet to discover and learn.

It was only after I started living in the college dorms that I realized how diverse my food palette was at home. Sure, I've upgraded to a newfound sense of freedom with no curfew and unlimited access to McDonald's caramel frappes after 10 p.m. But my meal plan downgraded to leftover take out, spaghetti, and whatever-is-left-in-the-mini-fridge stir-fry. Like many ABCs who are experiencing the college dorm life, I learned to adapt to the shifting food landscape. On some weekend mornings, I could be happily eating rice noodle rolls at Chinese restaurants with my parents. But by Monday night, I would be reheating leftovers in the crusty communal microwave.

During those 9 a.m. weekend mornings, my parents would drag me and my brother to eat morning dim sum. In Cantonese, this is called "饮茶," which directly translates to "drink tea." However, this tradition of eating dim sum is more than just drinking tea and eating chicken feet. This is where family, friends, distant relatives, and neighbors gather around a round table to catch up with the latest news and gossip. Conversations can range from this year's poor backyard crop yield to how so-and-so's kid got into Harvard and how the same so-and-so's second kid is popping pills.

It is at these local Chinese restaurants where one would get a taste of the tight knit and thriving Chinese community here in NYC. These morning dim sums are bustling, energetic, and the culmination of beautifully orchestrated organized chaos.

Upon walking into the restaurant and squeezing your way through a parade of families all waiting to be seated, there's a frazzled lady in a power suit holding a clipboard and a stack of loose white paper. You could hear before you can see her through the crowd. She may be five foot four, but she is efficient, commanding, and trilingual. Even with ten customers barking questions around her, she remains unflappable at a podium, belting out numbers on her microphone in Cantonese, Mandarin, and English.

"27 号 27 HO NUMBER 27!"

"Did she just call our number?" asked an impatient daughter-in-law. "She said number twenty, right?"

There could be 514 seats in the restaurant and every single one of them would be taken, including the highchairs. A table normally for five people could technically fit eight people with enough "scooting in" and "sucking in of the stomach." It also isn't an authentic dim sum experience unless there is a mother screaming at her kid to stop playing Minecraft on the iPad at every table.

These lively mornings at the Chinese restaurant are where I learned how to flag down *aiyis* (aunties) rolling around the food cart filled with delicious plates of 肠粉 (rice noodles), 糯米鸡 (sticky rice wrapped in bamboo leaves), 流沙包 (egg yolk custard bun), and other dim sum staples. The *aiyis* would place the bite-size dishes onto the rotating glass center table and put a stamp on a paper card that tracks the type of food ordered.

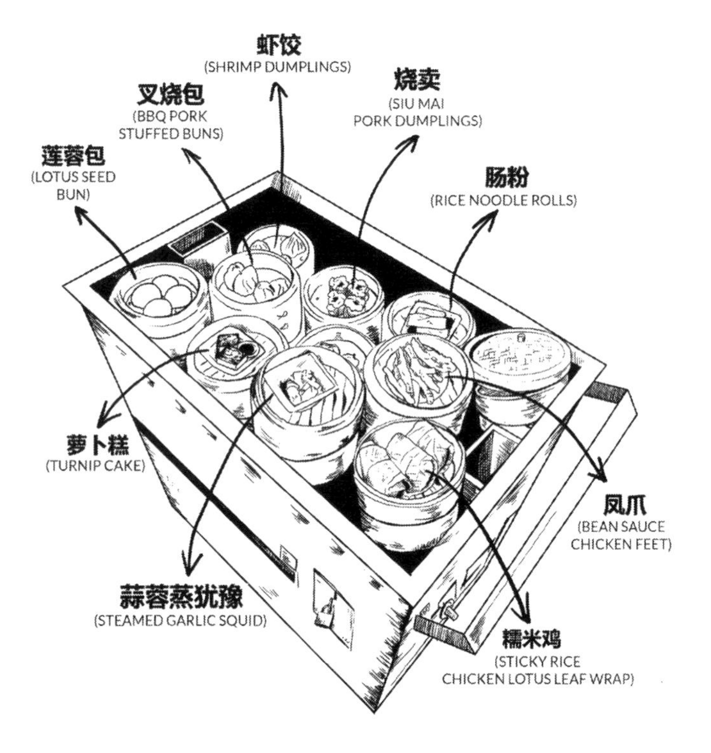

It is also in these bustling restaurants, where I learned about the concept of patience. The entire eating-drinking-chit-chatting process takes two to three hours, which doesn't even include the hour-long waiting time for a table. (Basically, the equivalent of my lunch break during remote work.)

I would spin the center glass table for another turn and rub my left temple. *Patience is a virtue. Patience is a virtue.*

After twenty-two years of being chopstick-fed radish cakes and dumplings, I learned a thing or two about proper Chinese dining etiquettes. Here are my three takeaways:

1. If someone is pouring me a cup of tea, you must use two fingers and tap it on the table next to the cup to signify thank you.
2. If another person, especially an elderly one, is picking food from the round glass rotary table, it is advised not to yank the glass table toward yourself. That last piece of shrimp dumpling can wait.
3. Most importantly, after two hours of eating the same food, you *must* fight over the bill when it is time to leave. It doesn't matter if the bill is ten dollars or if the bill is one hundred dollars. Scratching, yelling, climbing over chairs are all acceptable options. All means are necessary to justify the end goal: paying for bill. Otherwise, you would risk "losing face" and bringing shame to your family as someone who is stingy and belongs on the community shit list.

As much as I found comfort in eating homestyle Cantonese food and dim sum, the mild and sweet dishes didn't set me up for success in the outside world.

My embarrassingly low spice tolerance puts me at a disadvantage whenever I go to eat hotpot with friends. Hotpot is a traditional Chinese meal where raw vegetables and meat are dunked in boiling broth. It's honestly more of a communal experience than anything else. There's nothing more intimate than a family or friends sitting around a table waiting for a fish ball to float to the top of the boiling broth.

Typically, the pot is "split" into two different soup bases. On one side is the miso broth for my spice-intolerant weak ass. The other side of the Sichuan Mala hot and spicy broth for my friends whose life mantras are "Diarrhea comes with the hotpot experience—so embrace it." Since this is a family-style meal and my friends could eat from *both* sides of the pot, I am always left digging at the bottom of the pot for scraps and leftover enoki mushrooms. I predict that in the year 3071, teachers will be explaining the concept of survival of the weakest to the class and my headshot will be featured.

WHEN ANCESTORS EAT FIRST

Even with healthier style cooking of Cantonese dishes, canker sores still make uninvited weekly appearances in my mouth. Just as one canker sore was starting to dissipate, its cousin starts sprouting on the other corner of my mouth. My grandma says it's because I am 热气—"heaty," a condition in which the chi and balance in your body are thrown off by eating too many spicy foods. I am no dietician or nutritionist, but I am stubborn—so I continue to scarf down an entire twenty-five cent bag of salt and vinegar chips.

After hearing me whine about the canker sore, grandma would immediately run downstairs and start a batch of 凉茶 (a black herbal tea that counteracts the effects of *heaty-ness*). In its original recipe, 凉茶 is the type of bitter herbal tea that sticks to the back of your throat and lingers there until you wash it down with a Capri Sun drink.

But over the years, I convinced my grandma to add a couple bars of cane sugar to counteract the bitterness. It makes the herbal tea drinking experience less painful and cathartic. I also learned that if I closed my eyes and imagine

I am merely drinking a can of Coke instead, it makes the experience, dare I say, enjoyable.

In addition to the herbal tea concoctions, grandma would occasionally come upstairs to the second floor after making a fresh batch of pastries or food for the appropriate holiday.

Since my brother and I aren't well-versed in the lunar calendar and the Chinese holidays, we would have heated debates about this.

"It's the Zongzi holiday," I protested.

"No. It's the moon cake holiday," said my brother.

"That's a different holiday, dumbass."

"No, it's not, dumbass."

"Yes, it is—go ask Grandma."

In other households, one could sense there is going to be a big feast for dinner when they smell the aroma of their grandma's chicken pot pie or lasagna. But for me, especially during Chinese holidays, I know I am eating like royalty that night if I detect the powerful smell of burning incense.

My grandma would light up a batch of the incense whenever she is making an offering or praying to the gods and ancestral spirits. When that lingering smell of a burning incense travels upstairs, I know that meant that the steamed chicken, roasted pork, and stir-fried veggies are all waiting for me on the table downstairs...after the ancestors ate first.

Over the years, I've grown so accustomed to annual batches of 粽子 (sticky rice wrapped in bamboo leaves), herbal tea, soup connections, and moon cakes that I often forget Grandma is the last direct cultural link to the motherland in China.

Truth be told, before I formally started learning about the Chinese language and culture in college, I didn't know squat about the origins of specific Chinese holidays. Most of my primitive knowledge about Chinese cultures and their origin derived from the food my grandma made for the specific holiday.

At twenty-two years old, after living abroad in Asia for a year and graduating with a Chinese major later, I feel like I know so much yet so little about my own culture. Over the years, I spent most of my time eating the food rather than learning about the history and the origins. In a sense, there lies even a deeply rooted fear of losing a culture I never fully connected with.

I might not always remember the significance of a specific holiday or the specific proportions on how to make sweet and sour pork. But what I know for sure is that the customs and food that have been rooted into my existence during childhood would somehow feel empty without their presence.

No matter how many books and articles I read about the history and culture, my grasp on this aspect of my ABC identity still feels superficial. It is even more painful to know that with each new generation in America, a little bit less of my ancestral roots are being passed down. Eventually, morning dim sum in Chinatown will be replaced with family brunches in the East Village, herbal tea will be replaced with a cup of cappuccino, chopsticks replaced with forks, and the stories of Chinese customs will at most be a distant memory of the ancestors. I hope my grandchildren will be able to balance this duality between the old and new—that even if they choose to eat brunch over dim sum, they still equally value both sides of them and remember where they came from. I also hope that by the time my grandchildren get this book, I will have learned how to brew the bitter herbal tea concoction so they can get a taste of my own medicine.

TIME CAPSULE II

Read This to Embark on a New Journey

CHAPTER 3

Before the Sun Rises Again

Dear Rauful,

Do you ever wonder what would have happened if we didn't meet each other in high school? Better yet, what if our parents decided not to immigrate to New York? I would probably be a village girl living in rural China, while you would be a city boy living in Bangladesh. In that case, do you think we could still find our way home to each other?

I don't tell you this enough, but I am extremely thankful that you are beside me while we navigate these tumultuous early years of adulthood. Together, we shadowed surgeons in Lithuania to live out our *Grey's Anatomy* fantasies. We even scaled the Great Wall of China together in the sweltering heat of Beijing.

Thank you for being the only constant in the sea of ever-changing variables. You willingly took on the impossible, unpaid, and overworked role as my trustworthy mentor and confidante. I admire your adventurous spirit, your self-discipline, your desire to generate impact, and your determination to help others and leave the world in a better place than we found it.

It's funny that the moment you think you have your life plan figured out, the plates start to shift. How naïve it was for me to think that life will go exactly according to my five-year Excel sheet plan. They say that life is full of many unexpected surprises and opportunities around every corner. I'm just glad we were able to find each other around this one corner of Bedford Avenue and Campus Road. And just like that, that somehow changed our entire roadmap.

With love from your person,
Janette

WHEN IT'S ABOUT THE FORBIDDEN "D" WORD

In my household, there are many big "no-no's" and "off-limits" areas. But the top three foolproof ones are:

1. Wearing shoes in the house
2. Getting caught by my grandma for not drinking her soup
3. Dating before college

Like many female Asian children living in Chinese households, I've heard the phrase "You cannot date until college" one too many times.

"Right now, focus on your studies—not dating," my dad would say.

"I know, I know," I would reply with an eye roll and a complacent nod of the head.

From my parents' and Chinese families' perspective, it's understandable. They traveled all this way, from the other half of the world for me to get a solid education—not for me to get a solid dating life. Their second worst nightmare is probably finding out I am sixteen and pregnant, right next to "I'm dropping out of school to focus on my art."

I used to think that my mom was "too old" for having me at twenty-five years old. That is until I recently found out my grandma had my dad at twenty years old. Currently, at twenty-two years old, I can't imagine settling down until I am well established in my career and learn the difference between eggshell white paint and flat white paint.

Especially for those fortunate enough to live in developed nations, the timeline has dramatically shifted, especially for females postponing their marriage and having kids in favor of their career. However, what *hasn't* shifted (in my opinion) are traditional Chinese households and their attitudes toward dating. (That's right, Mom and Dad, I'm looking directly at you.)

Thinking back at my childhood memories, I vividly remember twiddling my thumbs over my hand-me-down Blackberry to change my male friends' names to more suitable girl names. "Justin" became "Justina" and "Daniel" became "Daniella."

I've learned early on to prepare for the worst-case scenario. In that case, it would be the time my grandma spoke to her friend whose sister's husband's neighbor supposedly saw me walking down the street holding hands with a boy. When that happened, it didn't just unfold, but it started to unravel into a downhill spiral. It was similar to the line-to-line reenactment of that scene from the movie *Crazy Rich Asians* showing a network of "Have you heard..."

A couple of hours later, after the dinner leftovers were packed into Tupperware for the next day's lunch and the dishes were washed and left to air dry on the kitchen rack, my parents were briefed on the latest news.

I was already upstairs, tucked away in my corner of the house, finishing the last bits of my seventh-grade creative writing project due the next morning. I beamed at the hodgepodge of different Word Art fonts, all underlined by a squiggly line with Crayola markers. I was proud to see my vision come to life.

Suddenly, the sound of my father's heavy footsteps drew closer as he stomped up the stairwell. A knot immediately formed in my stomach. I knew something was wrong.

The door slammed behind him as he bellowed out, "Janette, come outside."

I froze.

"OKAY!" I blurted out.

I jumped up from my chair, tripped over some clothes, and stumbled to the door.

As I gripped the doorknob with my right hand, I stood there frozen, replaying the 101 worst nightmare scenarios in my head over and over again. But the only scene that appeared was the one at the top of the "I'm fucked" list.

They knew.

I slowly turned the doorknob, afraid my hesitation already gave it away. My feet dragged behind me as I made my way down the hallway and into the kitchen where my dad has been standing. His hand rubbed against the bearded stubble on his upper lip and chin, his head looking down as if he were trying to count the number of specks on the marble table.

I was positive the neighbors could hear my heart pounding; it was trying to break free from my chest. I prayed...to a god...some god...all the gods for a miracle. Someone quick, ring the doorbell, call his phone, accidentally chop off a finger? I didn't care; I was desperate.

I walked up to the kitchen table pretending like I didn't have a clue.

He used that stern and assertive tone and said, "Grandma told me her friend saw you holding hands with a *boy*." He said the word *boy* with so much disgust, as if he immediately had to go rinse out his mouth afterward.

I began reciting my monologue. *Deny, deny, deny.*

"I don't know what she's talking about."

"I have no idea."

"Nope, wasn't—"

Dad interrupted. "Give me your phone."

I immediately burst into tears. "NO! WHY? NO!"

He slammed his hand on the table, and the house shook. "Give. Me. Your. Phone."

He was looking at me dead in the eye, but I didn't allow my eyes to meet his. I trekked back to my room and shuffled around, pretending to look for my phone. But I knew where it was. My hands immediately got to work. The ball at the center of the Blackberry device clicked away as I quickly deleted any and all questionable texts. It was probably something like, "What did you get for the answers to these questions?"

Click. Click. Delete.

Click. Click. Delete.

A few moments later, I returned to the kitchen table and handed my phone over, like I was some criminal being stripped of my possessions. For a second, I questioned whether I should just whip the Blackberry against the wall and say, "Oops, my hands must have slipped." But the thought vanished just as quickly as it surfaced. The thought of going back to my grandpa's government Tracfone that had monthly minutes terrified me more than getting my privacy invaded.

What followed was a twenty-five-minute speech and presentation about the dangers of dating early. My mom dutifully took the lead as head presenter and my grandma watched me as I wept quietly in the corner. After a couple of days of silent treatments hoping that the non-communication would resolve itself, the cycle reset and all was well in the Wu family household.

Word on the street is that many young people date early because they crave the attention that their parents are not providing them—but that's just a theory I heard somewhere.

WHEN WE REJECT THE ORDINARY

During my high school years, my eyes were set on one thing and one thing only: academics.

Maybe this was the result of external parental and societal pressures. Or maybe this was the result of a sudden realization that I had full-on manual control of my happiness and success.

After getting my heart tossed out the window like my annual New Year's resolutions to stop procrastinating, I realized my value and worth don't depend on someone else's happiness. This realization is revolutionary, especially in a society that profits off self-doubt and insecurities. Instead, by being consciously aware of my self-worth, I knew it was up to me to take control of my ship and steer it in the direction that could benefit my career, my interests, and most importantly, my happiness.

For the longest time, I bought into the fake Disney lies that said girls are stranded in a tower waiting for a prince charming to come and save them. Fuck that—I can save myself and ride off into the sunset on my mystical fire-breathing dragon.

The closest Disney princess I resonated with is none other than the warrior and savior of China herself: Mulan. This woman single-handedly (with the help of friends) pulled a Katniss Everdeen to save her father from enlisting into the Chinese army and oh, saved the fate of the nation as a side hustle. Mulan is the epitome of breaking free from misogynist ideals and Chinese cultural traditions—and looking like a top-tier badass while doing so.

Likewise, I understood I didn't have to complacently accept traditions for the sake of maintaining traditions. I realized I am the only one who can take control of my happiness and be the princess charming I needed for myself. I didn't need to find my other half. I *am* my other half. I needed to find someone who can accept me as a whole and push me to be a better version of myself every day.

This realization, coupled with a two-page list of high standards for my future partner was a recipe for academic success. No more distractions. No more "playing hard to get." No more settling for immature boys who only recently learned how to tie their shoes the year before. Instead, it was only me versus a truckload of AP classes that could boost my GPA and finesse my way into college.

Then everything changed ~~when the fire nation attacked~~ the night of the Arista and Archon school ceremony. Arista students are those who have achieve a 93 average or higher and Archon students have accumulated many hours of community service. In other words, this ceremony celebrates the overachieving ass-kissing students. And for that one night, students had to swap out their Forever 21 and American Eagle clothing for formal white-top and black-bottom attire.

It was around five o'clock on a warm spring night during my junior year of high school. My friend Victoria and I were walking toward the entrance of the school when I saw a tall, skinny-looking brown boy in the distance. I didn't know it at the time, but he was Bengali American. The boy was wearing a baggy untucked white dress shirt that was obviously taken from his dad or older brother's closet. Even though we both went to the same prison for three years, I had never seen him before. Yet there was something about his laid-back yet confident demeanor that piqued my interest.

During the ceremony, my gaze unconsciously gravitated toward him. I mean, he was one of the tallest boys in the sea of wrinkled white attire. It was impressive to land on the Arista and Archon list, but I remember noticing he was a part of the Arista group like me.

How...interesting...Perhaps he is different from all the League of Legend addicts and academically apathetic boys I've known.

Although I didn't agree with the education system's overemphasis on grades, I was smart enough to recognize when to defy the system and when to cooperate with the system—and I was wondering if this tall, skinny, brown boy was playing the same game too.

After that "interaction," I let that memory fade away without thinking too much about it. That is until senior year started, and someone walked into my Advanced Placement AB Calculus class.

I found out his name was Rauful (It rhymes with waffle). He still hates that joke to this day, but I would say it's better to be called Waffle than to be called Ra-fool. But at the time, I didn't think too much about it because I was more concerned with the 67 percent I got on my first Calculus test along with the crippling anxiety that comes with the college application process.

A couple of months later, my friends Jephany, Christine, and I created our own senior hoodie. The default senior hoodie used a font that resembled Chinese take-out menus. Not only was this offensive, but it was also a bold assumption I was willing to look like a walking advertisement for the neighborhood Lucky Palace Chinese restaurant.

The entrepreneurial side of us scraped together a quick Google Forms questionnaire to gauge interest. A couple days later, I noticed that in column A, row 67, I saw a familiar name that rhymes with falafel. I was going through the Excel sheet to follow up on students who gave me inconsistent information. For someone who is an Arista and AB Calculus student in the medical sciences program, I was surprised to find out that Rauful incorrectly filled out a simple five-question questionnaire. (I mean, how can you actually fuck that up?)

I sighed and quickly searched his name in the Facebook text box.

How do you spell his name again? Raful? Rafull?

The name Rauful Hossain appeared with 208 mutual friends.

I clicked on his profile, then clicked on his profile picture. He was standing in front of one of those Chinese trifold room dividers wearing a dark blue button-down shirt that looks more fitted than the white one he wore at the Arista Archon ceremony. His hair was combed but overgrown, seemingly caught off guard but still posed for the photographer who stuck the camera in his face at the last second. I scrolled down to view his profile (because why not, we all do it). It consisted of images from his track team meets; most are pictures of him, and his track teammates. *Cute. But lame.*

I clicked on the message button and my fingers twiddled over my laptop keyboard. I knew *what* I had to say, but I didn't think too much about *how* I was going to say it.

Should I say "Hey Rauful!"? Or does the "hey" make it sound like we are already best friends—when we're not? Does the exclamation mark sound too eager?

Maybe I should say, "Hi Rauful"? Or does that sound like the header of an email inquiry?

On the bottom right hand corner, the digital clock flashed 9:55 p.m.

What if he was asleep already? Oh, who cares, I doubt it. There's no way he already finished that AB Calc assignment yet.

January 28, 2016, at 9:56 p.m.

"raufulll

can you fill out the google forms link so I know your hoodie infoo"

I hit the enter key and hesitated.

Suddenly, a voice in my head said, "SHOOT YOUR SHOT GIRL!"

The other voice in my head said, "Nah, he's dumb—Can't even fill out a simple form. Save your Cupid's arrow."

A few moments later, I quickly typed out an alternative option and hit the enter key before I had a chance to backspace the message.

"or just tell me here so I can help you put it into the excel"

I sat back on my chair, threw my hands behind my head, then patted myself on the back with my right hand. *What a slick way to continue the conversation, Janette.*

A couple of minutes later, the seen message popped up. A series of blinking ellipsis followed. *Rauful Hossain is typing...*

Before my anxiety had the chance to warm up and kick in, he replied.

January 28, 2016, at 10:01 p.m.
"Whaaaaat didn't I do it?"

January 28, 2016, at 10:04 p.m.
I replied back.
"nopeee
okie I see it now"

I will spare the rest of the details because it is as nonsensical and cringeworthy as typical high school text message conversations. For the next month, we exchanged a lot of text messages in what we didn't know at the time to be the "getting to know each other" phase. Unexpectedly, we immediately clicked. Truthfully, it was refreshing to have a conversation with someone that didn't involve the question, "Hey, can I see what you did for last night's homework?"

From the subtle game of twenty-one questions, we learned about each other's fears, ambitions, and other 2 a.m. high school deep-talk conversations that safely tucked away before the sun rises again.

In between these conversations, I noticed all the qualities that made me gravitate toward him. He has a child-like curiosity, yet he exudes a rare sense of maturity at seventeen. He is confident but humble, outgoing yet reserved. He doesn't need my validation to understand his self-worth. Most unexpectedly, he is extremely impact driven while being anchored by his core values. We vibe on similar frequencies and even to this day, we are tethered to similar life philosophies. We are drawn to the same core values with a strong desire to create impact and do good, and a mutual rejection for the complacency of being "just ordinary."

While we are similar in many ways, we are equally different in others. He is a creature of habit, one who craves stability and reassurance, while I, on the other hand, am a creature of constant identity crises, one who thrives off spontaneity and endless possibilities. What I thought to be our point of weakness turned out to be our greatest asset. Over time, we learned to complement each other like yin and yang or like boba and tea.

Around mid-February 2016, there was a grand opening for a waffle shop in Chinatown called Eggloo. It was an elevated version of an egg waffle 鸡蛋仔, a traditional Chinese street food that literally translates to "little eggs." This snack is typically sold in a tiny cart on the streets of Chinatown. But instead of charging $1.25 for twenty pieces, Eggloo was charging upward of eight dollars to have the waffle stuffed in a cone form, topped with a spoonful of red-bean ice cream and the cavity-inducing toppings that my eight-year-old nostalgic heart desired—I didn't care. I am a sucker for sweets and I willingly handed over my wallet filled with the crisp bills from Chinese New Year.

I shared the buy one, get one (BOGO) grand opening promotion post with Rauful, hinting at the idea that *he* can buy one and *I* can get the other one. At that stage, I was dropping so many hints, but he was picking up none of them—except for this one. So, we took the hour-long train ride to Chinatown, stuffed our faces with some overpriced but delicious waffles, walked over to the AMC movie theater at Union

Square and watched *Deadpool* with awful seats near the front of the screen.

Yet in that dark theater room, with my neck cramping from being jammed in a 150-degrees upward position and my teeth gearing up to fight the incoming troops of cavities, I looked to my left and saw this skinny brown boy chuckling at some cheesy *Deadpool* pun. The movie screen illuminated his face, highlighting his high cheekbones and the corners of his jawline. I turned my head back toward the screen and smiled to myself, forgetting about the rest of the movie.

WHEN WE SAT IN THE DUSK LIGHT

Twenty-three days.

It took twenty-three days since our initial conversation for Rauful to ask me out—and I was a ticking time bomb. You can ask guys simple and straightforward questions like:

"So where do we stand?"

And they can reply with things like, "On the floor; what do you mean?"

By day seventeen, it was Valentine's Day, and I was impatient.

Then on February 20, 2016, we went on a bike ride. At the time, I owned a Schwinn mint hybrid cruiser. She had seven different speeds that could take you to the local farmer's market and help you get up the hills in Park Slope. With wide handlebars and a sloped frame, I didn't have to break my back every time. After I had convinced myself to buy a twenty-dollar straw basket, the bike looked like it had come straight out of my NYC-living-Cali-dreaming Pinterest board. She was a beauty—but heavy as shit at forty-seven pounds.

I loved biking for as long as I could remember. On my fourth birthday, my parents got me my first bike. It was

Barney-purple and magenta, which matched perfectly with my Barbie helmet. The best part was the bike handle streamers that flapped against the wind when I pedaled hard and heavy at ten miles per hour. My steering could've used some help, but I blamed it on constantly having to shift my weight between the left and right training wheels.

With this new ride, it was no doubt I was the cutest kid on the block. Looking back at old photo albums, there were twenty-three portfolio pictures of me with this bike. On the inside, I was ecstatic. But out of the twenty-three pictures, only one featured me without a stone-cold face of boredom.

Rauful and I bonded over our mutual love for this hobby. There is something liberating and adrenaline-inducing about biking. In later years, we would take annual two-hour bike trips from Brooklyn to Manhattan together. Rauful would be cruising up and down hills unbothered, while I would be panting and sweating through every pore on my body but loving every moment.

But that day, on Saturday, February 20, 2016, the weather was abnormally warm for winter. The kind of weather that by day, foreshadowed the early arrival of spring but by night, reminded me of why New Yorkers say, "It's mad brick (extremely cold) outside."

Rauful and I decided to take advantage of this weather and biked over to Brooklyn Bridge Park in DUMBO (Down Under the Manhattan Bridge Overpass). As the sun dipped down the horizon behind the Manhattan skyline, he popped the question and ba da bing ba da boom—we were now Facebook-status-official boyfriend and girlfriend.

I stared off into the distance, mesmerized by the city lights that illuminated the sky. I tried to focus my gaze on every lit-up window in the Manhattan skyscrapers and pondered about each of their different realities. Were they still grinding away at their standing desk and dual monitors? Perhaps they were shoveling some leftover Chipotle into their mouths before heading home, I wondered.

I zoomed out and tried to capture every passing minute. The setting sun painted a shifting landscape that made the city more and more mesmerizing with each stroke. Below us, the grass hugged our legs. To my left, Rauful was still entranced by the city's final act of transition into nightfall. Without the glaring light from the movie theater, I had a better look at his side profile. His cheekbones and his jawlines were his most prominent features. His cheekbones were higher than the stoner kid who spent half the class period "using the bathroom." His jawlines, strong and chiseled enough to crack open bottles. Yet, in the dusk light, his face looked soft and mature. I wondered again about the people inside each of the thousands of skyscrapers' windows—I wondered if anyone also said yes to a decision that could drastically change their lives.

A moment later, Rauful caught my gaze and smiled.

I leaned over and whispered, "Ah, don't you love light pollution?"

Little did I know that a technical glitch on a Google form questionnaire could not only spark the beginning of a relationship but also alter my entire life trajectory. But, to my high-school-senior self, what was more traumatizing than asking a teacher for a recommendation letter was how I was going to break the news to my parents. But that's a problem I delegated to four-years-later future me.

CHAPTER 4

And Then There Were Nine

Dear Mom and Dad,

How did you both do it?

It must not have been easy for you both to immigrate to a foreign country and attempt to raise two rambunctious American kids while instilling the values of Chinese culture. You tolerated my defiance, impatience, and stubbornness. (You can discuss who I inherited that from).

Back then, I perceived your "rules" and "overbearing-ness" as strict and irrational. Now, as I am growing older, I understand you were just trying to protect me—from the evils of the outside world, the big bad wolves, and especially the heartbreaks.

I think somewhere along the way, I also unconsciously learned how to protect you. Not in the same form of food, shelter, warmth, and safety, but in the form of withholding information. They say ignorance is bliss. In my case, the less you both knew, the more I felt like I was able to protect you from the additional stressors outside of your control.

We might not always agree on the same things, but I know you both want what is best for me and my future. I can only hope you continue to keep an open mind about our differences and beliefs about the world.

I hope you understand Derek and I are old enough to make our own decisions. But this doesn't mean we will abandon all the beliefs and values you've instilled in us. It doesn't mean we will abandon you. We will continue to carve our own paths, make our own decisions, make stupid mistakes, fail courageously, and fall hard on our faces. But we will remember to keep in mind what you've taught us: to get up, dust ourselves off, and try again.

I want you both to know this: You did the best you could with the knowledge you had at the time. I don't blame you for my shortcomings or faults. My only wish is for you to also believe that too.

With love,
Janette

WHEN THERE ARE NO FURTHER QUESTIONS

It was Sunday afternoon in May 2019, and I was sitting in the backseat of my dad's car as we inched through the traffic on the Brooklyn Queens Expressway. My parents and I drove out to Manhattan to get ramen at a restaurant called Wagamama. Usually, I avoid scrolling on my phone or read during car rides. I have a bad case of motion sickness and whenever I do anything besides stare out the window; it sends a direct message to my brain to regurgitate my eggs from breakfast.

But things were different that day because it was the day before my twenty-first birthday.

In a parallel universe, an alternative version of me would be interested in alcohol. I would gather ten of my closest girlfriends and we would all pretend like it was the first time that the elixir touched my lips. Then we would spend the night posing for pictures with me in a "21 and Fabulous" satin sash and a bejeweled plastic tiara. There would be a thick crease from the fold after it's been held hostage at my local Party City, but my alter ego wouldn't care—because it would be my twenty-first birthday and I'd be an adult now and no one could tell me how to live out my pageant queen dreams.

But in our current universe, this version of me is more interested in going to the DMV than intoxicating myself to numb my childhood pains, which is why this version of me is celebrating her twenty-first birthday at an all-you-can-eat sushi buffet. Because nothing gets me drunk like the thought of dunking my eighth piece of salmon sashimi in a pool of low-sodium soy sauce. Amen.

The previous night, my brother Derek announced he was bringing his girlfriend, Maxine, to my birthday dinner. Under normal circumstances, I wouldn't have batted an eye. But no, the news was alarming—not because he was bringing a plus one to *my* birthday party—but because I didn't even know he had a girlfriend in the first place.

So, when I found out, all I did was recite the five "W's" and one "H" that I learned from elementary school.

"Who? What? When? Where? How?" I yelled.

Apparently, every time she came over, I wasn't home. And every time I was home, she didn't come over.

I grilled my brother from across the room, hoping that I can activate our sibling telekinesis ability.

"Fine, whatever," I said to him.

And with that simple confirmation, Derek retreated into his room, and I was left with my twiddling thumbs.

I immediately swiped open my phone and texted Rauful: "You won't believe what I just found out."

Back in the car, I was dialing the number to a sushi buffet restaurant. I started making a mental count of the total number of people for the dinner reservation.

Mom, Dad, Derek, and me. That's four. Plus Maxine and her family, that's eight. Yes. eight people.

Even before I could process the words about to come out of my mouth, I blurted out,

"I'm bringing someone too—so that's nine people—" I paused.

From the backseat, I saw my mom's head nod of approval.

"—and he's a *boy*." I cautiously added, biting my tongue after the words slipped out.

I stared at the back of their heads, looking for a sign—*any* sign of reaction from the *B* word I just dropped.

"Okay," my mom replied.

One second went by. Two, Three. Silence.

"係你嘅男朋友啊"—"Is he your boyfriend?" my mom asked.

"Mhm," I replied, bracing myself for the impact.

Another second went by. Two, Three. Silence.

But there was no impact. No probing questions. No comments or concerns. No further questions. Little did I know that shit had already hit the fan. But the fan just wasn't turned on yet.

WHEN THERE'S A VERBAL DIVIDE

At Wagamama, we were quickly seated at high top tables with my dad across from me and my mom to my right. From my seat, I had front row seats to the west side of Madison

Square Park. I saw the occasional runner with a slick headband and questionable running form, and the neighborhood French bulldog taking their owners out for an afternoon walk.

After we each ordered our bowls of ramen, my mom suddenly turned to me.

“佢係唔係中国人啊?” —“So, is this boy Chinese?” she blurted out. Her tone was less probing than it was curious.

I hesitated. “He’s not Chinese...but he can speak Chinese,” I replied, treading lightly.

“Huh? 你係咩意思?”—“What do you mean?”

“He is Bengali—Um, his parents are from Bangladesh. But he can speak Mandarin.”

I looked down, avoiding my parents’ gaze. I could feel my hands starting to sweat, and I fiddled with the paper casing around the disposable wooden chopsticks.

“佢靓唔靓仔, 畀我睇下佢啲相”—“Is he handsome? Let me see a picture of him.” She said motioning her hand toward my phone.

I immediately breathed a sigh of relief. Before this moment, I was apprehensive about my mother’s reaction. She wasn’t necessarily the “bring home whoever you want, whenever you want” type of mom. If anything, she leaned more toward the other end of the spectrum.

I quickly scrolled through my photo album to search for a “parent-approved picture” until I found one of a selfie we took together at an art gallery.

Across from me, my dad remained silent. He didn’t need to say anything for the three of us to sense his disapproval. He poked at the bowl of ramen and suddenly said,

“你知道佢哋同我哋唔同个呵?”—“You know they are not like us, right?”

They.

The word paralyzed me to my core. This *otherization* of another group. The verbal divide between us versus them.

They.

The one word that makes us forget that beneath our differences in culture, religion, complexion, we are all humans after all.

Unconsciously, I gripped the paper that encased the disposable chopsticks. My thumb pushed up against the base and suddenly, the tip of the chopsticks pierced through the paper, revealing itself.

He continued, "佢哋信唔同嘅宗教, 文化都唔一样, 食物都唔一样"—"They believe in a different religion, a difficult culture, eat different food."

There it was again. They.

"So?" I was defensive, and my voice trembled. "We don't even believe in any religion!?" I added.

"我哋信佛教"—"We are Buddhists," he replied.

I rebutted. "No, we're not...Grandma is. I'm not."

"佢哋同我哋就唔一样"—"They just aren't like us," he repeated again.

WHEN WE CAN PRONOUNCE "SUPERCALIFRAGILISTICEXPIALIDOCIOUS"

Like many traditional Chinese households, my family would prefer that I bring home someone who looks like us. No need for translating conversations, explaining why shoes need to be taken off before entering the house, or explaining why red beans do not belong in any other dish other than desserts.

This is less about appearance and more about maintaining the harmonious flow of the family dynamic. Unlike American society, Chinese society has emphasized the collective group and family rather than the individual for thousands of years. Family is the nuclear unit of society in Chinese culture. Anything that threatens the stability and comfort of the household is avoided at all costs.

Chinese people also believe in "losing and saving face," a cultural concept that involves avoiding disrespectful actions or words. This concept is more than just ego, self-pride, or dignity. In fact, the words or actions of *one* individual will affect the relationship with others in the community. Not only is the action a reflection of the person but there is also an unspoken understanding that it reflects their family and friends.

It's always so difficult to explain this concept to my non-Chinese friends, so I will do my best to explain it through examples.

Let's say May works at an international Company X. Her real name is Xiao Mei, but she morphed her name into May to accommodate her American coworkers' inability to pronounce Xiao Mei but their ability to pronounce supercalifragilisticexpialidocious is spot on. Her American coworker, Jake, comes up to her and repeatedly asks her to help him complete a task even though the task is outside the scope of May's responsibilities (and pay grade). The conversation goes something like this:

Jake: "Hey May, can you help me record this transaction in our database?"

Xiao Mei: "Um...I don't think that I'm the best person for this job."

Jake: "Sure you are!"

Xiao Mei: "Um...I don't know, I'll think about it. Maybe you can ask Debra instead?"

Jake: "Nah, Debra is busy with her own work. Here you go—let me know when it's complete. Thanks May—you're the best!"

In this scenario, Xiao Mei didn't want to confront Jake by telling him that the task was not her responsibility. At the end, she didn't refuse it either because this confrontation would cause both parties to "lose face" increasing the tension in their relationship.

To many Americans, Xiao Mei's behavior seems detached, avoidant, and even uncollaborative because of her unwillingness to help her coworkers. But Xiao Mei's Chinese upbringing and values on social harmony are often misinterpreted by her American coworkers.

As I was growing up, this concept was unconsciously baked into my mind. This culture of beating around the bush, reading in between the lines, and tip-toeing on eggshells was exactly how I learned to operate in American society. Head down, thumbs up, avoid confrontation, and confront inner conflicts—all in the name of "saving face" for myself, and for others around me.

Essentially, since the family acts as one entity, the action of the individual influences the image of the nuclear family unit. To my western non-Chinese friends, I know how fucking bizarre this sounds. Imagine if I accidentally forgot to cover my sneeze in public. Some droplets from my sneeze accidentally sprayed my neighbor and ricocheted off their plate of food. A Chinese auntie from the other side of the room would jump to the assumption that my mother isn't a good parent because she didn't educate her kid on proper social etiquette.

Along the same lines, the act of bringing home a non-Chinese man would wreak havoc on the tight-knit Chinese community. Forget asking about the new boyfriend's values, aspirations, or zodiac sign; let's all jump to conclusions about how the parents allow the American public school system to destroy the child's family's values and neglect of Chinese values.

For as much as Chinese people value the entity of family, it's hilariously paradoxical of them to care so much about the opinions of those outside of their families.

WHEN THERE ARE THIRTY SECONDS ON THE CLOCK

The night before, I gave Rauful a short checklist.

- ☑ Buy six oranges.
- ☑ Prepare an English self-introduction.
- ☑ Prepare a *Chinese* self-introduction.
- ☑ Brace yourself for impact.

Over the many years of attending Chinese housewarming parties, I became a sponge.

Not only did I soak up all the family gossip, but I also absorbed all the necessary Chinese social etiquette to impress Chinese aunties and uncles. This is how I know one should *never* show up to another Chinese home (or any home) empty-handed. Fruits are the safest and best option. A box of chocolates that comes in a fancy metal tin container works too. There is a 95 percent chance that the recipient will re-gift the box at someone else's housewarming party, but that's beside the point. The point is in the small and kind gesture. A gesture that acknowledges you are a guest in someone's humble abode while upholding standard Chinese etiquettes. That's the golden ticket, baby.

I told all of this to Rauful, to which he replied: "Oh yeah, I know, we learned about this in Chinese 101, remember?"

"Fact. But hello," I countered. "This is not another one of our class role play scenarios."

To learn about Chinese culture via textbooks is one thing. But to experience it firsthand is another. This is the real deal, not your fifth-grade school play—this is Broadway bitch.

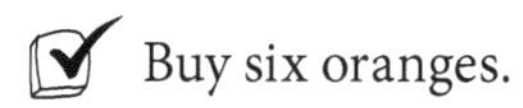
Buy six oranges.

Not two, because that will make you look stingy. Not four, because four represents death in Chinese culture, but six, because Chinese people love things that come in pairs.

☑ Prepare an English and Chinese self-introduction.

This is important. My parents, especially my dad, love formalities and someone who takes initiative. In Chinese culture, people strongly believe in the concept of filial piety, an important three-thousand-plus-year-old Confucian value that children must be respectful and in deference to their parents and elders. Similar to the housewarming gift, the self-introduction is a sign of respect to your elders and acknowledgment of Chinese culture's social etiquettes.

At that stage, there were only two things my parents knew about Rauful.

1. He is not Chinese.
2. But he speaks (Mandarin) Chinese.

They didn't know we had been dating for three years already. They didn't know about his capacity to be self-disciplined toward his goals. The goal was to make them love him as much as I do and see how much light and warmth he radiates. To this day, we are still working on that, but it's a group effort and I'm starting to feel like it's one of those high school "group" projects where one person carries the team.

This is why it was so important for Rauful to nail the Chinese self-introduction. I am a firm believer that language has the ability to break down barriers. It's one of the many reasons Rauful and I embarked on this Chinese learning journey together. We have witnessed first-hand how people immediately let their guards down when you speak to them in their native language. To reach over the aisle and let them know they don't have to conform to "This is America—speak English!" standards. To let them know they belong—equally as much as those that were born on US soil. By introducing himself in my parents' native language, I wanted my parents to feel comfortable with the idea that Rauful also belonged in our home.

☑ Brace yourself for impact.

The day before, I told Rauful to be prepared to answer rapid-fire questions.

"What are you studying?"

"What do you want to be?"

And other questions answered in the self-introduction, but active listening wasn't employed.

On the day of the meeting, I was sweating through every open and clogged pore of my body. I was less concerned about meeting my brother's girlfriend, Maxine, for the first time than I was about how my parents were going to react to Rauful.

At 5:30 p.m., Rauful drove up to the front of my house, right on time for the 6 p.m. meeting. Early = on time. I always commended him for his punctuality and my lack thereof.

"Rauful's here!" I announced to the rest of the house.

He stepped out of the car with a plastic bag filled with what looked like twenty-two oranges. The seconds that he took coming up the front stairs felt like hours, and I gestured him to hurry to the fuck up because my arm was getting tired of holding the screen door open.

They say first impressions are made within the thirty seconds of meeting a person. Some say fifteen seconds and others say seven seconds. But for the sake of giving Rauful more wiggle room, the clock started now.

Thirty seconds.

As he stepped inside, he handed the plastic bag of fruits over to my mom and greeted her.

"这是给你的小礼"—"Here is a small gift for you."

"Wow, thank you!" she replied, swooning over the deconstructed bag of edible arrangements.

Twenty-five seconds.

Mom opened the bag and said, "That's a lot of fruits! Oranges, apples, and bananas!"

Next up on the chopping block: Rauful meets Dad.

I stood off to the side, pretending to sift through the farmer's market that Rauful just brought over, but fully, actively, taking note of every gesture and words exchanged.

Twenty seconds.

Rauful walks confidently over to my dad and shook his hand firmly.

At six foot one, Rauful towers at least a head taller than my dad. Rauful also prides himself in his handshakes.

"Strong and firm," he instructed me one time. My handshakes waver between holding a newborn's tiny hands to squeezing a stress ball—no, in between, I never get it right—but Rauful always does.

Fifteen seconds.

Right on cue, Rauful began his self-introduction.

"Nice to meet you, Mr. Wu. My name is Rauful Hossain. 我的中文名字是何家佑。何是任何的何。家是家庭的家。佑是保佑的佑。"—"...My Chinese name is He Jia You."

In a Chinese self-introduction, it is common to "explain" the characters of your name since many characters phonetically sound the same. It's similar to the concept of homonyms in English (flower versus flour). Instead of giving a name like Karen that now symbolizes white privilege and entitlement, Chinese people like to give their children a Chinese name that contains an auspicious trait.

THE ANATOMY OF A CHINESE NAME

Surname + Given Name
In Rauful's case, his Chinese name is 何家佑.

何: Pronounced "Huh?"—Last Name English Translation: He
家: Pronounced: "Jia"—English Translation: Family
佑: Pronounced: "Yo"—Like "Yo, you just cut me in line." English translation: To assist and protect. This character is also used in the Chinese word for "to bless."

Ten seconds.

Rauful continued his self-introduction about his college majors, which like me, are also human biology and Chinese. He continued to explain his career aspirations.

Truthfully, I cannot remember the rest of their conversation or my dad's reaction. I remember hearing my dad chuckle when Rauful began his Chinese self-introduction, but as for the rest, I can't recall. I was too caught up in peeling all the stickers off the oranges and apples than "eavesdropping" in their conversation.

After that conversation, I introduced Rauful to my brother, Derek and his girlfriend Maxine. Even though Maxine was my brother's age, a.k.a. two years younger than I was, she reminded me of my younger self. She is quiet and reserved, not saying much but still present in the room. She was also ABC—her family from Guangdong, China; she also spoke Cantonese.

Before we left the house to stuff our faces with $33.99 worth of all-you-can-eat sushi, we all stood around the island table, exchanging small talk about the weather.

During most of the conversation, which was mostly in Cantonese, my dad directed his questions to Maxine, occasionally cracking his infamous dad jokes. With each joke, I did a half-assed translation of the joke for Rauful, and he lightly chuckled at my failed attempt.

I knew this wasn't going to be easy. I knew my parents weren't going to welcome Rauful or the idea of an interracial relationship with open arms—but I was determined.

This is the part of the story where you might expect the "turning point." The climax of the story that warrants and invitation to Rauful by my parents over for close family hotpot gatherings. But the truth is, currently, five years into the relationship, we are still working toward that goal.

If you could imagine that storyline your seventh grade English teacher drew on the chalkboard, you will see that for this part of my story, I am still in the "rising action" stage—and we are only going onward and upward from here.

CHAPTER 5

A Leap of Faith

Dear Mom and Dad,

You both probably didn't even know I was formally studying Chinese in college until summer 2018—when I announced I was planning to jet-set to Taiwan, the land of bubble tea and night markets. Truth be told, I purposely kept a lot of the details about my academics out of our conversations. Based on my horrible track record, I was going to drop my Chinese major just like how I dropped ballet lessons, piano lessons, violin lessons...you both get the point. This is why I didn't want to get your hopes up about learning Chinese again.

I already know what you both will say when you read this: "We sent you and Derek to Chinese school, but you both didn't want to go!" Yes, I admit. You both were right, and I'll get more into the effectiveness of these Chinese school classes later on.

During the three and a half years of formally learning Mandarin in college, there were days where the lack of progress would frustrate me to the point of no return. In those moments, I wish you both had forced me and Derek to continue Chinese school—or even encouraged us to learn

Spanish or another language while our young brains were primed for language acquisition. But I know you both did the best you could with the given resources. Besides, I gained a newfound appreciation for language learning now that I am older, so 多谢爸爸同妈妈—thank you Mom and Dad.

识讲些少中文嘅女 伍霖莉

Your daughter who knows how to speak a bit of Chinese, Janette

WHEN IT'S A PIPE DREAM

It all began in the spring of 2016.

Unbeknownst to me, I was about to make a decision that would change the entire trajectory of my college career—or my entire life, if I can be bold enough to say that at twenty-two. I am certain that even when I am eighty-two, wrinkly, and rocking back and forth in my rocking chair, this story will still be a testament to time. But in the meantime, Asians don't raisin, right?

It was a Monday night in April 2016, or maybe it was a Tuesday night. Honestly, to many high school seniors, weekdays are all lumped together and the only things that matter all begin with the letter S (Saturday, Sunday, and summer).

"You got mail!" said Dad, hollering from the other side of the house. From the echo of the sound of the enormous thump on the kitchen island table, I knew it could only be one thing. Finally, the day has come. My college admissions package from *the* Macaulay Honors College at Hunter College. It would eventually take a couple months before I could spell Macaulay correctly without messing it up. I would repeatedly say "A" before the "U" to myself while I was filling out the college acceptance forms in high school. I immediately sprinted out of my room and into the kitchen. I received my acceptance by email a couple weeks prior, but it wasn't *official* official until I teared open the manilla packaging.

My dad glanced over from across the pile of mail he already tore open—many of which included mine and my brother's mail.

"What's that?" he said, raising his eyebrows. From the curiosity in his eyes, I could tell it took great resistance to not open this package. Just like the concepts of paying for shipping fees, the model minority myth, and curfews after 8 p.m., the concept of invasion of (mail) privacy is not something that my parents believe in.

"Oh, nothing important," I shrugged.

Here I was, face to face with a glossy midnight black folder. On the cover sits a slightly crooked, rounded corners sticker saying Macaulay Honors College at CUNY Hunter College. The background of the sticker looked like the school entrusted a kindergartener with a purple crayon to do some mediocre job at shading. But in the school's defense, this wasn't an arts college. Instead, it's the Ivy League of the public city college system, where students can get the financial and academic support they need to graduate debt-free.

Ah, yes. "Debt-free," all Asian parents and educated millennials' favorite "D" (and "F") words.

Regardless, I was entranced by the glistening black folder. It wasn't one of those cheap one-cent paper ones you get at the Staples "Back to School" sales. No, no, this one didn't crumble with a mere loose-leaf inside. Instead, it's one of those sturdy, non-flimsy ones, strong enough to hold two pounds of pamphlets and my self-worth inside. It isn't a lot, but it will do. There's nothing better than reliable stationery.

Out of all the club brochures inside like TEDxCUNY or Habitat for Humanity, I was drawn to a particular one with the name of Hunter College Chinese Flagship Program in bright red bold letters.

It was a simple-looking flyer, printed on normal eight-and-a-half-by-eleven-inch copy paper. I quickly skimmed through the flyer...intense program...training to become fluent in Mandarin...group sessions, tutoring sessions, cultural activities...study abroad. *Jackpot.*

I admit, all their selling points were enticing. I could learn about a new culture and connect with people from all around the world. But the key selling point was the opportunity to study abroad in Taiwan and Mainland China, a.k.a. the motherland.

I closed my eyes, daydreaming about all the bubble teas I get to drink. Milky drinks. Fruity drinks. Even the weird ones with the cheese foam top that, according to the laws of science, shouldn't blend together with milk or tea. But in Taiwan—it does. Because it's Taiwan—the motherland of bubble teas. I sighed again.

I opened my eyes again and read the last sentence on the bottom of the flyer, immediately striking a needle into my study abroad bubble.

"Only twenty-five students get in each year."

It was a loud and confident disclaimer. This wasn't even written in fine print, so I knew the program had nothing to hide. Even after a year of taking AP Statistics and endless practice SAT questions about probability, I never got the hang of it. But even I know that when considering the statistic of Hunter's general undergraduate population of nearly 17,000 students, no calculations are needed to conclude the odds were not in my favor. I tucked the flyer behind the other pamphlets and closed the folder.

The next day, I brought the holy folder to school with me to show Rauful. At that point, he also decided to attend Hunter College with the Yalows Scholars Program, a program designed for students on the medical or research track. This is also known as the track for students who already have their next ten years mapped out with arrows and twine linked inextricably on a bulletin board. Rauful had also applied to Macaulay at Brooklyn College for their BA/MD program but got rejected (their loss, in my opinion). We were both disappointed we didn't get into our dream schools, but glad we were able to spend the next four years together in one. I knew he was one of the few people who I could confide in about this space-limited Chinese Flagship Program. It was a decision that weighed heavily on me.

To provide some context, my relationship with Chinese (the language and the culture) is complicated to say the least.

I am the definition of the stereotype that ABCs 识听唔识讲—ABCs who can understand Chinese (Cantonese, Mandarin, Taishanese, etc.), but they aren't able to communicate verbally. Since my grandparents were the ones who raised me in the beginning years, Cantonese and Taishanese are considered my first languages. But when I entered the American public school system, English slowly but surely replaced my Chinese speaking abilities. As a result, my Chinese withered away into a conversation basis.

"嗯，嫲嫲，我食饱啦。"—"Yes, Grandma, I've eaten already."

"爷爷，功课一啲都唔难。"—"No, Grandpa, school isn't hard at all."

I had to give some credits to my parents. They tried to bridge that language gap that inevitably comes with assimilating into American culture. When I was in elementary school, my parents sent me off to Chinese school at the Chinese Consolidated Benevolent Association (CCBA) in Chinatown, Manhattan. This after-school program was a perfect two in one combo meal for my parents working full time. Not only did the after-school program offer pick-up service for me and other ABCs after school was dismissed, but the program also assisted with homework and taught Cantonese learning classes. However, the only thing that I remember is the time where I purposely pushed my pencil over the edge of the desk claiming that I "dropped it accidentally." Then, while leaning over to pick it up, I stealthily ate rice noodles that hid in my school desk. Afterward, I sat myself back up, wiped the soy sauce dripping from the corners of my mouth, and prepared my eraser for the next drop-off.

During those elementary school days, I was speaking English to my friends and teachers and occasionally speaking to my grandparents at home. My Chinese was still salvageable. Yet somehow, even with me secretly eating noodles during class time, I was able to win first place in a Cantonese story-telling competition for my grade. First place!

Back then, I was young enough to be immunized from fears of judgment and embarrassment of standing on stage. Maybe this is where my need for external validation began. Somewhere along the lines, I learned to equivocate my value with the glory of a shiny "Made in China" gold-plated trophy. Then I took that and just ran with it.

I was also young enough to absorb the language like a sponge. Nowadays, it's so ridiculously easy it is for a child to "lose" a language because they can barely string together a couple sentences in Cantonese today, let alone a whole story.

After transitioning into middle school, my parents fought our language deterioration by hiring a private Chinese tutor for me and my brother Derek. They somehow persuaded my neighbor's parents to join, too. Our neighbors' kids were also ABCs. One is the same age as my brother, and the other was a couple years younger.

To this day, I don't remember what we learned in those sessions or even if we had learned Mandarin or Cantonese. However, what I remember is the private tutor asking me if she could take a nap on my bed because she was "too tired." She was probably in her twenties and naively didn't know that her tutoring gig also doubled as a Saturday afternoon babysitting gig for four children.

Without my parents' home, I was the oldest and therefore, head of the household. I eagerly granted her request not only because I knew how hard she was working to get all four of us to remain seated for more than fifteen minutes but also because I knew I had to work *harder* to allot more Nintendo DS time with my fellow classmates. It was not an easy task to defend my title in first place for the Mario Kart battles, but it was definitely easier without distractions from learning Chinese.

After graduating middle school and moving on to high school, there was less emphasis on salvaging the lost cause of learning Chinese and more emphasis on preparing for the standardized tests to get my overachieving ass into college. I eventually accepted the fact that I was never going to be able to connect back to my roots again—which is why I was so hesitant to apply to the Chinese Flagship Program at Hunter College.

Disregarding the fact that only twenty-five students get in every year, I was reluctant to apply to the Flagship program because learning a new language at eighteen years old is extremely hard—almost impossible. It doesn't take a scientist, researcher, engineer, or anyone with common sense to tell you that it's a pipe dream to learn a language from beginner to fluency especially when Chinese is deemed one of the hardest languages to learn in the world. And after four years of waving my hands up and down to mimic the tones of the Chinese characters and constantly comparing myself with other native speakers, I can verify and confirm this shit is fucking hard.

Back in the peer tutoring room at Midwood High School, I narrated my entire cons list of *why I shouldn't learn a new language in college* to Rauful. I whipped out the now crinkled flyer from my book bag.

"There's just an extreme time commitment...and just the fact that language acquisition isn't as easy at seventeen." Rauful nodded in acquiesce.

"And what about —"

He suddenly stopped me before I could name the rest of my excuses. "What about—we give it a shot? We won't know if we don't apply."

"*We*?" I asked again to make sure my brain wasn't playing tricks on me.

"Yes, *we* could both apply and see what happens," he said nonchalantly, as if he just agreed to pick up some eggs at the store for me. He continued, "Besides, I would like to learn a new language and study abroad too."

I couldn't tell if he was just trying to gain brownie points for the leading role of being the encouraging boyfriend or if he genuinely thought we had a chance when the odds were literally twenty-five of 17,000. But his optimism was a refreshing juxtaposition to my glass half-empty attitude.

And just like that, with a new partner-in-crime in hand, the devil's advocate in me threw up his hands in surrender screaming, "Yeah, why the fuck not? Let's see what happens."

WHEN WE WERE RUNNING MATES

Looking back at the list of cons I've written down, all of them were viable top contenders for "Best Excuse of the Year." But the last con—the one that Rauful stopped me from admitting out loud—was hidden deep in my subconscious mind. Fear of rejection. This recurring theme would show up multiple times throughout my life. After enduring a gruesome chain of rejection emails from my top college choices (that's right, NYU Dental, I'm looking right at you), the thought of another email headline of "We are sorry to inform you that...." automatically tied a knot in my stomach. So, when this decision to apply to the Flagship program came around, I was extremely wary and protective of my already bruised and beaten down ego. My justification at the time was: You can't get hurt and rejected again if you don't apply in the first place, right?

This time, I put a Band-Aid on this ego and fervently type up my flagship application essay with Rauful at a nicely air-conditioned Starbucks in Williamsburg. In the following weeks, after gathering the courage to press submit on the application, we anxiously waited for a reply email (and by we, I mean just me, because Rauful was a calmer than New York City pigeon, unbothered by the crowds of tourists and honking taxis).

When we finally got a reply, we were summoned for an interview at the Flagship office with Rauful's at 3 p.m. and mine at 3:30 p.m. I thought it would be a good idea if we both showed up together with our arms linked as if we were each other's running mate. I was determined to let the Flagship Office know that we come as a package deal and in this combo meal, instead of a side of fries and medium soft drink, you would get to check off the "diversity" box for Rauful, my Bengali boyfriend, and the "heritage speaker" box by yours truly.

In the days leading up to the interviews, we had to prepare a short introduction in English and another language of choice. I entrusted one of our good friends, Victoria, a fellow Cantonese speaker whom I have known since middle school, to do God's work by patiently listening to mine and Rauful's self-introductions. As expected, Rauful delivered an effortless self-introduction in Bengali while I, on the other hand, fumbled and mumbled through my Cantonese self-introduction, sprinkling in the occasional Chinglish (Chinese and English) commentaries. She gave me helpful suggestions, but all of them went down the drain when my nerves took over during the actual interview.

On the day of, I put on my best outfit that screamed, "I'm a college student." It consisted of a thrifted long-sleeved black blouse with floral detailing paired with a dark navy Zara midi-skirt that flowed down past the knee. Lastly, I sealed the look together with a pair of uncomfortable black flats with zero ventilation. I trusted this outfit. It was safe and modest. Hopefully, it conveyed the message that "I am a professional, but I can still be fashionable." My running mate, Rauful, wore a pair of neon blue basketball socks with his dress shoes. I was so appalled at this outfit choice that I recommended not wearing the socks at all for his interview.

This was my second time stepping foot into one out of the four Hunter buildings. The first was when I was invited for an interview for the Macaulay Program way back in November

2015, which felt like a complete and utter disaster that ended with me crying afterward in the Hunter bathroom. But this time was different. I had a running mate, and we marched up there to the fourteenth floor (and by march, I mean wait fifteen minutes in line for the elevators).

We circled the perimeter of the offices until we finally found room #1425. I checked the time on my phone.

2:55 p.m.

Right on time.

Being early is on time. Being on time is late. This is not a motto I followed word to word, but it makes a great lesson at the end of a children's fable.

I did three swift and assertive knocks on the door. A Chinese woman with short, layered hair and rectangular framed glasses opened the door and was visibly shocked to see two smiling high schoolers peeking into the small corner office.

"Oh, you're both here together," she said. She introduced herself as Hu Laoshi (Laoshi means professor or teacher in Chinese) and welcomed us both.

Rauful went first and even behind closed doors, I could hear him turning on his charm to win over Hu Laoshi. Along with his calm composure, he always had a way with words. He was assertive yet respectable in a humble manner that makes the listeners eager to hear what he has to say. However, on the other side of the door, I was sweating profusely and pacing up and down the narrow hallways. I was proud of myself that I remembered to put on extra swipes of deodorant to mask the burst water pipes situation occurring in my armpits. I was too nervous and on edge to even eavesdrop on their conversation, and what felt like three hours later, I heard feet shuffling from inside the room. Rauful casually stepped out with a grin stretched on his face and mouthed the words, "I got in."

Immediately, my anxiety levels, and sweat glands kicked into overdrive. Now it was my turn on the chopping block. I tried to walk in confidently and unfazed, showing more teeth to Hu Laoshi than what she probably asked for and sat down on the warm seat across from Hu Laoshi. (Thanks, Rauful for your kind gesture.)

Until that point, I didn't realize there was another person in the office. She was an older lady with oval glasses and short black hair that fell at her shoulders. She reminded me a lot like my grandma. I could tell she was one of the immediately likable people who smiled with her eyes. In the interview, I thought it would be a good idea to start off my English self-introduction with "I am a cup-half-full type of person," to which Hu Laoshi chuckled a little at this unexpected and cringey introduction. I just *had* to be different and deviate from the "My name is..." introduction. After that, I braced myself for the worst part of the interview: my Cantonese self-introduction.

Before this interview, I was never taught how to formally introduce myself in Cantonese. Never during the failed attempts at Chinese school and never during our limited sessions with the "very tired" private tutor. Whenever I would meet a new relative, my parents or grandparents would make the introduction for me, and I would obediently reply with "Hallo Yiyi (auntie)" or "Hallo SookSook (uncle)." Anything besides that was uncharted territory and the hours I spent watching Cantonese TVB Hong Kong dramas didn't prepare me for this.

After thirty seconds of reciting a paragraph that Victoria helped me memorize, Hu Laoshi asked me something in

Mandarin and I shook my head. She turned to Chao Laoshi and said, "Oh, so she does understand a little bit of Mandarin." Looking back, I probably shook my head, not because I was answering the question but because I didn't understand what she was saying. Hu Laoshi then started explaining details about the program and she could tell I looked like I wasn't processing the information even though she was speaking in crystal clear English.

I interrupted her and sheepishly asked, "So…does this mean I got in?"

"Yes...you did!" she exclaimed.

I then made an awful squealing noise and everything she said after that went in one ear and out the other. I couldn't contain my excitement because I knew this was a new chapter, the start of something new (cue the *High School Musical* soundtrack.) Finally, this was the universe's way of saying thanks for walking that grandma across the street three years back.

Afterward, Rauful and I celebrated by going to a bubble tea shop nearby. We exchanged stories from the interview and sipped our not medium but *large* taro bubble teas. After endless college decision emails that begin with "We are sorry to inform you...," we were both jaded by the commonality of insincere rejection emails—which is why we laughed about how odd it was that we found out about the decision on the spot.

After a quick Google search, we also discovered that the sweet grandma sitting in the corner during the interview was Chao Laoshi. She was the Director of the Chinese Flagship Program and Director of the Chinese Language Department at Hunter. She was the equivalent of first-class priority seating, and I, the bathroom seat behind row fifty-eight in economy. Upon that realization, I backtracked to see if I made some embarrassing commentary during my interview. Perhaps I said something I regretted—but it didn't matter. Rauful and I daydreamed about all the potential adventures abroad and how in a couple years from now, we will sip bubble tea in the place where it all began.

People never believe me when I tell them that some skinny brown boy I met in AB Calculus my senior year of high school pushed me to reconnect with my roots and learn an elusive language, and the best part was that he voluntarily chose to embark on this journey with me, unknown of the struggles that lay ahead and the rewards yet to come. And all it took were years of mediocre Chinese-tutoring, some half-assed self-instructions, and a leap of faith to quiet those subconscious fears.

TIME CAPSULE III

Read This to Hear My Inner Thoughts

CHAPTER 6

Call Me by My Name

Dear Mom and Dad,

Do you ever wonder how other people perceive you?

Mom, you may see yourself as Angela, a manicurist and business owner. But do you ever wonder if your customers refer to you as *that* Asian immigrant lady who does my nails? Dad, do you wonder if your former coworkers ever remember you by saying, "Oh yeah, he's *that* Chinese IT guy."

You might be thinking "Oh, Janette, you think too much about this. Just focus on yourself." But hear me out.

During the winter break of my freshman year of college, I took an "Introduction to African Diaspora" class. This crash course jammed a semester's worth of material into three weeks. In one of those long three-hour classes, I learned about the term "double consciousness" from W.E.B. Dubois's book *The Souls of Black Folk* (1903). Dubois used this term to describe his Black experience in a white-dominated society; ever since, the term has been expanded to include other racial minorities like ourselves.

"Double consciousness" is the idea that you are looking at yourself from the perspective of other people. The world "sees" us through the nerdy sidekick character in movies, the stereotype as a docile model minority, the distinct smell of our homemade lunch, the heavy accents, and more. But that's not who we see ourselves as. We are much more multifaceted and complex than that.

This concept didn't sink in until I started becoming more aware about myself and my place in the universe. Even though growing up in NYC has made me hyperactively aware of my surroundings, I didn't realize the existing divide that comes with how the world sees me versus how I see myself. As I grew older, I learned more about the world at large and the institutionalized barriers that are in place to prevent people like us from overcoming them. Because once we learn about what's hidden underneath the rug, we can't unsee it. Maybe one day, we won't have to worry about how my actions or inactions can be a totem for our race or background. Thank you both for coming to my TED Talk.

With love (and righteous indignation),
Janette

WHEN COMFORT IS SUBJECTIVE

When I was younger, I remember feeling envious of my friend's parents and families who could speak fluent English without any indication they were immigrants. Although my father could speak English fluently, his slight Chinese accent immediately revealed his multilingual background. My father was able to speak English and three dialects of Chinese: Mandarin (the most common form), Cantonese (the second most common, especially in the Canton or Guangdong province, Hong Kong, and Macau), and Taishanese (a rural dialect from my family's hometown in Taishan, Guangdong).

Similarly, my mother, is also able to speak the three Chinese dialects. As for English, after spending nearly two decades handling well-off Park Slope customers as a nail technician, she could carry herself just enough for small talk. I regrettably felt embarrassed by their Chinese accents and occasional grammatical errors. She would often adopt Chinese grammatical structures into English. No matter how many times I corrected her, "I don't get it" is still "I do *not* get it." Although now, I wouldn't even notice the mistakes or when I do, I would jokingly laugh about it. This wasn't always the case.

I was fortunate my father didn't need my help to pay the bills over the phone at a young age. But I do know many children of immigrant families had to grow up early and do all the adulting stuff in their childhood years. It's difficult, especially when these children are full-time students and breadwinners for their families.

When I was growing up, I remember overhearing my dad's phone conversations from my room at the other end of the house. By the other end of the house, I mean, just a couple yards away. We lived in a two-story home in a not-yet-to-be-gentrified neighborhood in Brooklyn. All the homes on my block had the same layout. These houses shared a wall with the houses on the left and right.

I lived on the second floor with my father, mother, and brother. My grandparents lived on the first floor. The door on the second floor leads into an open floor kitchen, living room, and dining room. Then a short hallway that led into one bathroom and three decent size bedrooms. I would provide the square footage of my home but measuring how "big or small" a home is based on this metric is subjective—plus I have no idea except for the metric that my parents use for determining a good home: "long-ness" or the physical length of the house. The (also subjective) metric I prefer is comfort. Sure, it may be a seven-minute walk to the nearest station or an hour train ride into the city, but I was comfortable.

On the days that I overheard my dad's phone conversations, I remember putting my ear against the door of my room. It has already been ten minutes of him following the commands of the automated machine.

"Sorry, can you repeat your full name? I didn't quite get that."

My dad sighed and repeated himself again, "J-un M-ing."

He stressed the "juh" sound in "Jun" and pressed his lips together to enunciate the "mm" sound in "Ming."

He tapped his pen impatiently on the table, with each tap signifying the number of complaints he will unleash onto the AT&T representative.

After a moment, the robot lady replied, "Hi June-Ming, please hold for a representative."

The soft dialing of the phone hummed along with the next representative on the line unaware of the wraths of hell my dad was about to bring into that conversation.

A few seconds later, the representative dialed into the call and started reciting the usual script of asking about the same information my dad already provided to the robot lady.

Dad immediately went off. Something about this random charge and that additional fee. Something about international calls and other hidden fees. He spoke in a stern, loud, and assertive tone. It's his "I've already lost my patience with you, but I don't want to make a scene in public" voice. I was at the receiving end one too many times when I accidentally snapped at him in public.

But in this conversation, he was in the comfort of his private home—so he made a scene. At the end of that call, Dad got what he wanted. The hidden fees and charges were dropped, and I could only imagine how traumatized that AT&T representative was.

As I leaned against my bedroom door with my hands cupped around my ears, I found myself in the role as a terrified bystander. Is this something that I would have to do when I grow up? That the only way to get what I want is to demand it? That I would get taken advantage of if I don't assert myself, or even worse, pay for those hidden fees? Did he raise his voice because he was genuinely upset, or was he doing it because he was fighting against the stereotypical image of Asian men being passive or docile?

With my back against the door, I reflected on how this situation could've ended up differently.

I thought about the immigrant families unwittingly paying additional fees every month. The ones that wondered about the upcharge but aren't tech-savvy or fluent enough to put up a fight with the nefariously bureaucratic companies. I also thought about how the robot lady butchered my dad's name on the phone.

When my dad first immigrated to the United States, he legally changed his name to "Johnny." When I was younger, I remember feeling perplexed at the name on his old passport. I was already shocked the passport didn't say "Dad," but it startled me even more to see some "white person" name on Dad's official document. A few years later, he legally changed it back to his birth name. "I just didn't really like it," he replied when I inquired about the switch back. I accepted his answer, but I can't help but wonder if my dad would've had to repeat himself on the phone had he kept the name "Johnny."

It's funny how there can be so much weight in the identity of our name. Even before we learned how to hold a spoon in our tiny fist, it's one of the first things we all learn to say. When we had to acclimate under the pressure of a standardized testing system, it was the first thing we filled into the bubbles of the test scantron. Finally, without giving the slightest number of fucks for being narcissistic, it's also the first thing we look for when we beeline to the keychain section of the souvenir shop. Our names are personal and unique to us—until Gmail tells us the name is already taken—so we settle with wujanette27 or some combination of the name.

The significance is even greater for our last names. On one hand, last names represent our legacy, lineage, and line of origin. This is one of the reasons why Chinese families prefer to have boys, due to their ability to pass on the family name. But on the other hand, last names also allow outsiders to make immediate stereotypical assumptions about your background, personality, and even work ethic.

In my parents' case, perhaps they were afraid their birth names would amplify the stereotype that goes along with the immigrant with the accented English. Maybe they just wanted to avoid the "Where are you from?" conversation. Even today, my mom tells her customers to call her Angela, instead of her legal name, Xiao Yan. I understand and respect why they chose to do this—but at the same time, this name change doesn't sit right with me. It feels like a forced act of assimilation, a waving of a white flag, a form of accommodation to make *others* feel more comfortable in your presence. But to my parents, and others who adopted a "Starbucks name" or "reservation name," it's worth it to avoid a repeated explanation.

But in that moment, while I was terrified at the booming sound of my dad's accented English, I was glad I didn't have to be the one barking or receiving orders on either ends of that call. I was comfortable—and so was my dad, when he cut ties with AT&T and received the next month's billing statement from T-Mobile.

WHEN IT'S PIZZA DAY

Even when my dad was giving friendly reminders in the car that I am Chinese, it was still difficult to fully accept that fact when everyone else around didn't accept it. Besides, you can't really expect an elementary school child to willingly embrace her Chinese identity when Little Jakey, the white kid who only ever had burger and pizza, scoffs at your homemade packed lunches. At first sniff, Jakey already had two fingers pinching his nose and had asked the kid next to him to scoot over more. He then had the audacity to point his booger-infested finger at my mom's homemade fried rice with Lap Churng.

"What is thaaaattt?" he squealed, and pointed at my Tupperware container.

"It's fried rice," I replied.

I looked down and fluffed the rice with my metal fork, unaware that my other hand was subconsciously reaching for the lid.

"No no no, I mean *that.*"

I knew he was referring to the Lap Churng but was wondering if he would start turning blue if he kept pinching his nose. I poked at the stiff red sausage and fluffed the rice around it again, hoping the rice could somehow mask the unwanted smell.

A couple seconds later, I gave in and said,

"Oh, that's Lahp Churng."

He stared at me blankly, and I reflected his stupid look back at him.

"Lap... What..."

"Lahp Churng."

He stared at me again.

I let out a sigh, snapped the Tupperware closed and said, "It's preserved pork."

Growing up I had so many variations of these conversations, each varying in responses ranging from "EWWW" to "What's that smell?" With each passing day, I ate less and less of my homemade meals sometimes packed with pork and cabbage dumplings, and my all-time favorite 糯米鸡. This savory sticky rice mixed with veggies and shredded pork or chicken is beautifully wrapped and tucked together with a lotus leaf. At some point, I surrendered and opted for the school lunch that specialized in the trifecta blend of dry, bland, and innutritious food.

Yay, another "pizza" day.

I stared at the soggy piece of reheated dough and started picking off a corner of the white Styrofoam tray. The "pizza" was coated in a layer of depressing half-burnt mozzarella cheese and bland marinara sauce. And it was served in a boat-like "pizza dough" that resembled a maxi pad. Everyone knows that pizza should only come in two shapes: the triangle and the square Sicilian slice (from L&B's Spumoni in Brooklyn only). Even in elementary school, I knew how sad this lunch looked. And I was supposed to wash it down with some one percent low-fat Elmoo milk? I'll pass.

As much as I hated school lunch, I hated explaining my packed lunch more. Yes, I was afraid of being laughed at for eating smelly food, but what I was even more afraid of was the wrath I would get from my mom or grandma if they found out I slam-dunked my perfectly edible lunch into the trash can.

Outside of constantly having to hide the packed lunches from both my life at school and at home, I had to battle with "Hey, chink!" and "ching chong" remarks creatively paired with the stretching of the eyes. When I was younger, I would visibly express my frustrations by rolling my eyes and making a 180 turn to walk away from their clown-like behavior. But now, I realized I shouldn't have given them the satisfaction of knowing that their hateful words were another reason to reject the Chinese side of me. So, on some days, I would put on a poker face and walk right past them. However, on other days, especially on days when my buttons were pushed too far and the top thing on my agenda were to pick a fight, I would march up to them and give a taste of their own medicine.

However, these stories about "smelly" packed lunches and racial remarks aren't breaking news. I'm certain that the majority of other ABCs or children of immigrant families like myself can retell some version of their own stories. But I want to point out that just because these stories are common, it doesn't make it acceptable. It's easy to laugh about these memories ten to fifteen years later. But at least in the moment, an action as seemingly innocuous and playful sits deeper into the young minds of children. Teach children to embrace the culture and cuisines of others. Educate them about how bullying can shapeshift into many forms other than name-calling and racial slurs. And most importantly, stop feeding our children that fake pizza crap. America is already the laughingstock for gun regulation, healthcare, and education, just to name a few. At least make sure that pizzas are the right shape, for fuck's sake.

WHEN GOD BLESSED AMERICA

In line with the topic of "Shit that ABCs Had to Endure," my fellow ABC friends will understand the frustrations that come with hearing the questions: "So where are you *really* from?" or "But, what are you *really*?"

I get this question at least once a week from "curious" people. The conversation goes something like this:

"So where are you from?"

"Here," I replied.

"Here where?"

"*Here* here. Brooklyn, New York, America...*here.*"

"Oh...but...where are you *really* from?"

"My family is from Guangdong, China."

He stared at me blankly, and I reflected his stupid look back at him.

"I'm Chinese," I added.

His face suddenly lit upon realization as if he discovered some rare exotic peacock wandering around the streets of New York.

"Ohhhhhh I knew it. I knew it. Got it. Got it. You a pretty lil' thang, aren't you? God bless you baby. God bless America."

I forced a half-smile and walked away, feeling his eyes glued on my back.

Yes, God Bless Freakin' America.

Sometimes I wonder if I'm of those people who won the jackpot lottery but were never informed to officially claim it.

How many "good luck heads up" pennies did I pick up in my past life to be born a woman and an Asian American in my current life?

Every day, I wonder if I had accidentally walked out the door with an "Unsolicited Attention Welcome" sign on my forehead. Because no matter how often I powerwalk like I got somewhere to be and someone to meet, I will always be seen through the lens as an "exotic," sexually desirable, passive, docile, and obedient Asian American woman. So don't call me baby, call me by my name.

After years of having these conversations, I've learned to perfect my craft of making these types of encounters as short and painless as possible.

"So where are you *really* from?"

"I am from here, Brooklyn, New York. My family immigrated here from Guangdong, China. So yes, I am Chinese. But I am also American. No, I am not interested in hearing about your Asian fetish. And no, I don't support eating dogs. I know I'm a pretty lil' thang and don't need you to remind me. Have a blessed day and GOD BLESS AMERICA!"

CHAPTER 7

Lost at Sea

Dear Mom and Dad,

Have you ever heard of the term 'ABC'? The Chinese translation "美国出生华裔" might jog your memory. ABC is short for "American Born Chinese"—children born and raised in America with Chinese ethnic background. Truth be told, I don't think that the term "identity" comes up often—if at all, in our conversations.

Identity is how you "see" yourself; it is the core of who you are. Mom, you may see yourself as not only Chinese, but also as a mother, daughter, friend, and cousin. It is the thing that distinguishes you from the rest of the crowd. Yet at the same time, it's also the thing that makes you feel like you belong in a larger community. Because even if all of your material possessions were stripped away from you, you'd still have this and family to hold on to.

When I moved to the motherland for a year, I thought I could at last resolve this constant ABC identity crisis. But to my surprise, I discovered I don't feel completely at home in China either. In reality, home is not limited to a place or country but where you are with your loved ones. Yet I still choose to stay and live in America because this is the place that we have called home for the longest. This is also the place where you have planted seeds, put down roots, and started a new chapter in our family legacy. By immigrating to America, you've given me the greatest gift of all—the freedom of opportunity and choice. This is the place where me and future generations have the opportunity to choose, not between "only American" or "only Chinese"—but both.

Now that I'm growing older, I'm beginning to recognize the superpower that comes with this ABC badge. I'd realize I am part of a new wave, a hyphenated blend that is unapologetic, courageous, and willing to break out of stereotypes and create our own mold. One willing to honor culture and tradition without blind devotion or adoption. A new generation that is multidimensional with expensive lifestyles that can justify eating twelve-dollar avocado toast. I hope you know that after you are gone, I will continue to plant seeds, cultivate stronger roots, and tell our story.

From your avocado loving ABC daughter,
Janette

WHEN IT KEEPS ME UP AT NIGHT

Attempting to explain this identity topic is like the unboxing of one of those Matryoshka Russian nesting dolls. Once I think that I have reached the core of the issue...surprise! Out comes another issue. This story is complicated, but I will try my best to take the past twenty-two years as an ABC and vacuum seal it into this chapter.

For most of my life, I felt inexplicably torn between the Chinese side of me and the American side of me.

On one hand, when in America, I am not "American enough" because of my Chinese background and the "smelly" homemade lunch. When Americans ask me, "What are you?" I reply, "I am Chinese. But I was born *here*, in America."

On the other hand, when traveling abroad in China, I am not "Chinese enough" because of my upbringing in America, my skin being too tan, and my subpar Chinese abilities. When Chinese natives ask me, "What are you?" I reply, "I am American." It's funny how I feel more patriotic about my American side when I am not physically in the country.

Ultimately, who I am doesn't match up with the predetermined image of what society makes me out to be. Being an ABC feels like I am lost, drifting in the middle of the Pacific Ocean waiting for a coastguard from either country to come and save me.

"Janette? What kind of name is that?" a Chinese coast guard would say as he puts down his binoculars. "She must be one of those bananas—yellow on the outside, white on in the side—born into a Chinese family but raised by the whiteness of American culture."

Another guard would chime in. "Her skin is also way too dark to be one of us. I bet twenty yen that she can't even write her Chinese name. Let the Americans claim her."

On the other side of the ocean, an American coastguard would scoff and say, "Her last name is Wu? Must be Chinese. Ugh, do we even have to save her when she might bring over the Chinese virus?"

"And isn't she a model minority?" another guard added as he retrieves his life raft. "You're telling me model minorities never learned how to swim? Let the Chinese claim her."

At the end, both countries are throwing their hands back and saying, "Nope, not one of us. Moving on..."

This identity topic resurfaced within the class discussion with my fellow heritage speakers at the Princeton in Beijing (PIB) program. My classmates were all raised with some form of Chinese background. At a minimal, Chinese ancestry was embedded in their DNA sequence.

One classmate was originally born in China but was adopted and raised by a white family in California. Another classmate's parents had immigrated to Peru, so she was born and raised there—now she attends school in California. Although the majority of my classmates have grown up in different metropolises across the United States, we were all sewn together by the golden thread of Chinese heritage. While my classmates and I were attempting to unpack this heavy topic, we each made the case for ourselves.

Everyone around me was contributing meaningful insights until I was taken aback when the classmate next to me said, "I only identify as American." I remember feeling perplexed and even slightly offended that she didn't identify as Chinese-American like the rest of us. She further explained that because she grew up in middle America, her family was one of the very few Chinese families in town. Growing up, she was constantly bullied for her Chinese background, which forced her to embrace and identify only as American.

The more I think about this encounter, the more confused I get about finding clarity amid the "identity" chaos. What I know for sure is that I never got to live life in the shoes of my fellow classmates. Their experiences are unique and personal just as her decision to identify as American. By doing so, she was not neglecting her Chinese ethnic side. Instead, her identity merely reflected her past unique experiences.

This whole identity thing sometimes keeps me up at night. It will be 2 a.m., and I am wide awake, staring into the darkness of my room and using all my strength to resist checking my phone for the seventh time. Sometimes, I recall that one cringey event that happened way back in 2010 and other times, I would think about how we are all just little specks of dust in this enormous universe. Just little specks of dust thinking about that one time a kind waitress said, "Happy Birthday!" to me and I replied, "Thank you—you too!"

After I shake off the memory and convince myself to stop dwelling on the past, I circle back to the thoughts that only seem to come to light when the rest of the world is fast asleep. What is identity anyway? Does it *really* matter? Isn't it just some label, social construct if you will, that makes it easier for others to classify and lump you into a stereotypical group? Should I look beyond identifying myself as Chinese, American, or a hyphenated blend of Chinese-American?

Will that stop others from making assumptions about me, assumptions that society has already instilled in them? Is "identity" just another way to further divide our society and separate us into "us versus them" or is it a way of comforting ourselves to maintain our sense of culture, heritage, and individuality by identifying with the motherland that some of us have never even been to? Or is it something more?

I don't know the answer to these questions. I've always operated in that "in-between" and "lost at sea" gray area, reluctant to choose a side. Partially because neither side will fully embrace my presence. Partially because of the fear of "lack of wholeness" if I end up on either side.

Perhaps this is just a coping mechanism to peel off a concrete label and comfort ourselves from the abstract feelings. That's why I chose to hyphenate the label of "Chinese-American"—to recognize that regardless of how hard society tries to instigate division, I can still choose to remain whole.

WHEN I WANTED TO BE JESSICA ALBA

Before the days of digital streaming where everything, and anything, is on demand, my house had a DVD copy for the superhero movie *Fantastic Four.* (Story, 2005) I would peel open the plastic case and click the plastic center to unlock the CD. Carefully, I would balance the fragile donut of a disc and blow off any residue dust before sliding it into the DVD player. I understood that every scratch meant one less time that I could watch the movie again.

Yes, I had watched the movie four times that month but perhaps this time, the ending of the movie would change.

This was a classic Marvel superhero movie, and one could already guess my answer to the question: *If you had one superpower, what would it be?* No, I didn't want to be the Mr. Flaming Hot Cheeto, or Mr. Spaghetti Arms, or even Mr. I Like to Smash Things When I'm Angry. So, by process of elimination (and lack of female representation), I wanted to be Jessica Alba. Even more than wanting her pristine blonde hair, I wanted to have the power of invisibility.

When I was younger, I looked forward to the imaginary days that I could sneak into Dave and Busters after hours and steal all the raffle tickets I could stuff in the training bra that I got from Kohls. Oh, the imaginary days when I wish I could sneak into the school and recalibrate the SMART board like I was a computer wizard who saved the school from a ransomware attack.

But nowadays, as a more practical young woman, if given the chance, I would use this power to do good. For example, I would skip the airport security line, movie hop and watch the movie from the projection booth, snag a bucket of popcorn without paying $11.79, sneak into the flight deck and start pressing random buttons while screaming "WEE OO WEE OO."

So, the power of invisibility was my go-to answer—until Ali Wong one-upped me with hers. In her book, *Dear Girls*, Ali revealed she and her then potential boyfriend, now husband wanted the superpower to speak all the languages in the world.

Of course—why didn't I think of that?

Who needs the power of invisibility when I can simply cajole my way into the movies or the Swiss International cockpit? When I read Ali's book, I thought about all the exposure I was fortunate to have with other languages. A little bit of French, Italian, Spanish, and Latin in middle school. Two years of Latin and Spanish in high school. (Don't ask me how much of that I retained, but that's beside the point.) Four years of Mandarin in college. Then of course, Cantonese, Taishanese, and English in between the gaps of the past twenty-two years.

As I am filtering through the years of experiences, I can't help but fixate on the negative memories. The lunchroom scenes and interactions with ignorant adults were inevitably imprinted onto my impressionable younger self. Ultimately, they all influenced how I perceived my Chinese-American identity.

When I was younger, I assumed how I perceived myself should be aligned with how society perceived me to be. I assumed qualities of my Chinese language, culture, and heritage were meant to be hidden behind the curtains or shoved underneath the rug. These qualities were designed to be weaknesses by default—mere flaws in a system that upholds the dominant "English only" American patriarchal society.

With every racial remark and "innocuous" stereotype, I learned to channel my inner power of invisibility, to hide aspects of myself, rather than embrace them. I learned to switch my language, behaviors, and even personalities around others, as I learned to associate shame with our family's background.

Now that I am older, more self-aware, and *less* impressionable, I've realized that what I perceived to be weaknesses were actually my greatest assets and secret weapons. Little did I know that I already had access to this "superpower" through my Chinese-American background while growing up in the melting pot of New York City. It was around this time that I began to recognize the untapped "power" of coming from a bilingual culture and background. For most of my life, ABCs, and others like me caught in the mess of the in-between, tugged on every limb to join the dark side. Yet all this tugging made me forget ABCs have been training for the real world their entire life. We are equipped with the knowledge of the nuanced understandings of multicultural backgrounds, knowledge that is increasingly needed to bridge our globalized society.

WHEN IT'S DIFFERENT SIDES OF THE SAME COIN

It was a long time coming, but I can now proudly say at twenty-two years old that if someone asked me this question today, I would say I identify as a Chinese-American or an ABC, American Born Chinese. As cliché as it sounds, the past four years of formally learning Chinese have allowed me to reconnect with my ancestral roots. I knew there was more to my culture and heritage beyond learning about the Great Wall of China and the Chinese Exclusion Act of 1882 in my history textbooks. Even more so, currently, there is more to learn beyond the politics that clouds the media about America and China relations.

When we really peel back the political and society's stratifying layers, what we find at the core of it all are human beings, yearning to connect with others and feel understood by others. We can facilitate this through language, and it is through learning Mandarin Chinese that I realized we are not so different after all and my Chinese and American aspects are just different sides of the same coin.

Nowadays, the adult "Jakeys" in the world may scoff at me eating chicken feet during dim sum at Chinese restaurants, but no worries; that means there are more for me and my stomach. And you know the famous saying: "A chicken foot a day keeps the doctor away."

While I still have to assume the full-time positions as translator, interpreter, and negotiator, there are fewer feelings of shame, frustrations, and embarrassment involved. Instead, they are replaced with feelings of pride and empowerment. Part of this newfound sense of empowerment comes from my role as a spokeswoman for my grandparents. However, the main reason for these newfound feelings is because I get to stand as a witness and be the voice for my family that has been silenced since they stepped foot into this country.

I will admit, this inner identity tug-a-war gets tiring after a while. It's capable of draining your energy yet simultaneously keeps you up at night past 2 a.m. But after twenty-two years of drifting along with the dead debris in the middle of the Pacific, you realize you've taught yourself how to swim all this time and can even save yourself.

CHAPTER 8

That New York State of Mind

Dear New York,

I have a confession to make.

Before I explain, I want to thank you for being so good to me for the past two decades. You've given me overwhelming love and support in the forms of opportunities and resources. You've stayed up all night and didn't even sleep because you were worried sick about my 2 a.m. whereabouts. In actuality, I was wandering around Grand Central with friends after we had just stuffed our faces from Boneless Thursdays at Buffalo Wild Wings. You have nurtured me to be the person I am today, and this is why you deserve to know the truth. I want you to know that it's not you; it's me.

For the past couple of years, I got into multiple...entanglements. I've flirted with other cities, cheated on you, and dare I say, even fell in love with some of them. Some of them were short-lived like the last-minute "Weekend Getaway" to Chicago, or my two weeks "Family Trip" to Vancouver and Alaska, or even my month-long "Career-Searching

Experiment" to Lithuania. These are nothing in comparison to the nearly year-long stay in China. It may seem like I had left on a whim without any form of a goodbye text or letter, but that trip was actually three years in the making. The truth is, although these trips were for vacation and career purposes, they were also a form of escape from you, and I'll explain why.

I've always had an itch to chart the uncharted territory, to travel, and meet new cities, new countries, new people, and experience new cultures. I desperately yearn to fill in the gaps between what I learned about the city from travel guides and the actual reality of the city.

If left untreated, this travel itch then turns into a nasty rash and trust me, there is no cream for it. However, I discovered that every time I get the chance to escape you, whether it is seventy miles up north for a day hike or 7,000 miles away in China, the itch subsides. Eventually, the novelty of this new place fades and I always end up running back to you.

New York, you've accepted me for who I am, let me in, and shared all you had to offer, even those in the hidden corners of the city. Your fast-paced life and attitude constantly push me outside of my comfort zone, and I am eternally grateful for that. This is why you will always be my forever home, but you are not my *only* home.

From a tourist in her own city,
Janette

WHEN I AM ONE IN EIGHT MILLION

"So, where are you from?" she asked.

My new classmate looked at me all bug-eyed, and I resisted the urge to tell her she reminded me of a cartoon anime character. I paused and held my breath.

This conversation can go down two rabbit holes. I quickly pull out the *where are you from* tree diagram from my mind map archives.

According to my calculations, based on my prior experiences, this question can result in two follow-up questions:

A. No, where are you *really* from?
B. WOW, *the* New York City?

I released my breath and said, "Um...New York...City?"

"WOW, *the* New York City?!"

Oh, thank God.

When I was living abroad, my classmates would immediately jump to crazy assumptions whenever I bring up that I am from the city.

"Wooooooow. So, what celebrities have you bumped into? Do you live on Park Ave? Do you see Broadway shows every weekend? Eat dollar pizza every night? Have you met any young, broke, and starving artist who is still trying to 'make it' in NYC?"

Their faces would then light up. Their curious eyes would widen, and pupils start dilating in anticipation for my response.

I would give them a sheepish look, hoping my hesitation would mentally prepare them for disappointment.

I can't blame them, though. With movies like *Sex in the City* and *The Wolf on Wall Street* on the big screens, it's hard not to assume that everything and everyone in New York is covered with flashing lights, faux fur, and men in suits. But in actuality, the reality couldn't be further from the truth of what it is really like to live and grow up in this city.

Truth is, I rarely notice celebrities in the streets because they do an impeccable job at blending in with native New Yorkers. (The key is to look unamused and uninterested.) I don't live on Park Ave, but I do live *near* a park. I don't watch Broadway shows, but I do watch couples air out their dirty laundry and intimacy issues on Broadway Ave. I do eat dollar pizza every *other* night. And yes, I do meet young, broke, and starving artists. In fact, I see one every time I look in the mirror.

The reality of New York City, at least for me, is far from what is depicted in the big screens. Many small-town-big-city people come to this city expecting rainbows, unicorns, and a fuck ton of glitter and glamour. But when they are confronted with fearless taxi drivers, daily harassments from the neighborhood catcallers, and a literal pile of shit in the corner of the subway station, they wonder what they have gotten themselves into.

I think unmet expectations are part of the reason people who didn't grow up in NYC do not stay in NYC, which is fine with me because that's one less slow walker I have to dodge.

But at least to me, NYC is more than just a city. It is a living and breathing organism with its eight million people acting as mini powerhouses of the cell. This is one of the most diverse and multicultural cities, and one can catch a glimpse of the world just from its five boroughs. This organism of a city thrives by feeding off every dreamer's ambition, perseverance, and dedication to their goals. Native New Yorkers have grown up with low expectations about this city, so nothing—even the pile of shit on a subway platform can phase them.

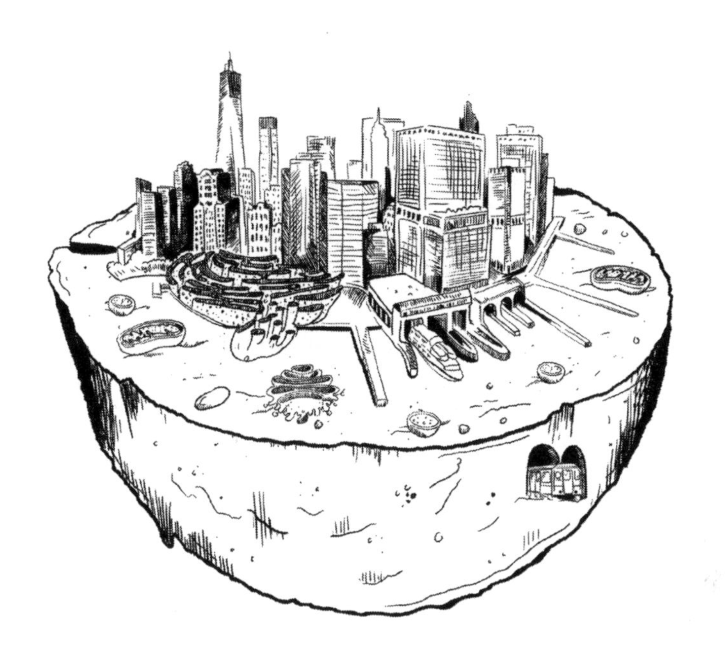

At this organism's heart and core lies Times Square. In a city of eight million people, 7,999,995 of them hate Times Square. I am one of the five who don't. Many natives would go to great lengths to avoid this lit-up Christmas tree that is a tourist trap. But for me, I purposely make an effort to walk through the heart of the city.

I would stand smack in the middle of Times Square with the red staircase behind me and the thousands of people around me. In the distance, I see an Elsa character mascot from Frozen. She is taking a picture with a naïve tourist holding a selfie stick with a backpack strapped on their chest. To my left, a naked cowboy is strumming his guitar in tune with the honking yellow taxis. Above me, gigantic billboard screens that make my sixty-inch TV look shameful. To my right, an aggressive Elmo is attempting to panhandle me for twenty dollars a picture.

Further off into the distance, I could see what used to be the headquarters of Toys "R" Us. It is replaced by a Gap and Old Navy store. Ah, nothing brings joy and a smile to my face than the thought of fast fashion and the exploitation of workers.

Before the store closed in 2015, I remember marveling at the gigantic fully functioning six-stories-high Ferris wheel located inside Toys "R" Us. Yes, you read that correctly, a whole ass Ferris wheel *inside* a building. Whenever I need a spurt of inspiration, I think about the inventor who had the courage to propose this Ferris wheel idea to the Toys "R" Us executive board.

There is something invigorating about being surrounded by five stories of flagship stores and millions of TV pixels that engulf the Square. The seemingly impossible doesn't feel so out of reach anymore. Here in Times Square, I can feel the pulse of the city and all I want to do is absorb all its beauty and energy. Somehow, this city can make eight million people feel like they are someone but also no one at the same time. It is this anonymity that galvanizes its people to swim against the current and eventually become more than just a face in a crowd.

WHEN IT'S SHOWTIME

Someone once asked me, "What do you love about New York?"

Off the top of my head, I said, "The people, the 24/7 shitty but accessible subways, the parks, the fast pace, the bluntness, the anonymity, the hustle and bustle, the food...definitely the food."

The beauty of living in this melting pot of a city is having the options of indulging in five-star restaurants or a six-dollar lamb over rice from a halal food cart. During my undergraduate studies, most of my meals were from these street food carts. It was cheap enough to fit within a college student's budget and filling enough to prevent my stomach from performing whale mating calls in class. It's also heartwarming to know I am supporting the businesses of other immigrant families also just trying to survive out here in these city streets.

For these carts, we all had our own Michelin star rating system. Similar to the Michelin rating guide, we judged carts based on consistency of food and value for money. Is the lamb over rice 10/10 the first time? What about the second? Third time that week? The answer should be D. Yes, all the above.

As for the value for the money, we must ask ourselves, "Does the one-dollar increase justify the free pita or drink that is included?" "Did I have a memorable experience with attentive service when the halal cart guy kindly asks me "White sauce? Hot Sauce?" Again, the answer should be D. Yes, all of the above.

Within this very much alive and breathing organism, the New York city transit system would act as the veins and arteries. New Yorkers have a love-hate relationship with the subways.

On one hand, we love the 24/7 service, the accessibility, that the subways interconnect every corner of the city. On the other hand, we hate paying for the spiked-up fare only to experience the same mediocre service, avoiding the unknown sticky substance on the subway floor, and sucking your stomach to get into the subways during rush hours. However, the only thing that is consistent about the NYC subways is the delays. There's almost an unspoken rule that one should add at least fifteen minutes to their commute. The bat signal for delays comes in the form of the train operator's muffled voice.

What I heard:

"Ladies and Gen...*something something*...delayed...*eye roll*...brakes...*sigh*...as soon as they can...*something something*...for the inconvenience."

What he meant to say was:

"Ladies and Gentleman, this is the conductor speaking. We are delayed because our automatic emergency brakes have been activated. Crews are working to get us moving again, as soon as they can. We apologize for the inconvenience."

I caught the eye roll of a middle-aged lady sitting a couple seats away. We gave each other "the look."

After the discontinuation of the middle school cheese bus service, I've ridden the subway enough times to give and receive this "look." I can attest to the fact that I have connected with strangers on the subway more than I have connected with some people in my life. It would be 9 a.m. and everyone on the train is sitting in silence with the guided meditation voice of the operator saying, "Stand clear of the closing doors please." This is until we arrive at Atlantic Avenue, and the bubble is suddenly bursting with the sounds of "IT'S SHOWTIME PEOPLE!" You could hear everyone in the subway cart let out a sigh. This was not what I meant when I said I wanted to see an off-Broadway show.

A couple of tall, slim teenagers file onto the train. One of them is holding a large stereo. He's the "hit the play button" guy. His job description also includes hyping up the current performers with the occasional "OKAY!" "YEAH YEAH!" Once the train door closes, the stereo guy doesn't waste any time before the train arrives at the next stop in forty-five seconds.

Hip hop music pounds out of the stereo and another member starts swinging around the subway pole, balancing his cap on his nose, and hanging from the subway ceiling railings...with his feet. After fifteen seconds, he hands the reins off to his teammate and he performs some more gravity-defying hat tricks and some bone-breaking dance moves that make me question how he unlocked that flexible joint function in his body. Keep in mind that they can do all of that while balancing on a moving train.

For a first-time traveler in New York, it's impressive. For a long-time New York native, it's still impressive. Bad timing, but still impressive.

During the performance, I would look up to try to sneak a peek at the subway sign but being careful to avoid eye contact with any of the performers. Instead, I caught the eye of another unlucky fellow subway rider. I attempted to send a Batman signal with my eyes screaming, "Help me!" and his eyes misinterpreted my message because his eyes screamed back, "Your feet are on the sticky stuff, stupid."

He was right. A can of what I hope contained soda was happily rolling down the subway cart, and it was leaving a trail of sticky substance in its destructive path. I immediately apologized to the can for the inconvenience and moved out of its way.

And with that said, my new stranger best friend, and I ended our conversation with a mutual nod of respect as we both synced our movements by tucking in our legs and lowering our heads for the showtime performers.

"WHAT TIME IS IT?" screamed the extremely optimistic performers.

"It's 9 fucking a.m." I mumbled underneath my breath.

"I SAID WHAT TIME IS IT?" they asked again. These guys were persistent.

"*It's showtime…*," I mumbled.

Don't get me wrong; I appreciate the hustle of these showtime performers. It takes a lot of courage, skill, and strength to be able to swing yourself up the railings while balancing a cap on your nose on a moving train. On days when the show isn't scheduled for 9 a.m., it's actually a nice break from the conversations with my own thoughts in my head. Especially when my commute to the city is over an hour, I end up logging in a lot of time with myself and my thoughts.

WHEN ENOUGH IS ENOUGH, STOP AAPI HATE

The many years of growing up in New York City have forced me to grow a tough skin. This tortoise shell was put to the test, especially in the year 2020. This year lifted the rug for all things including but limited to police brutality and accountability, shortcomings of the American healthcare system, climate crises, and so much more. Social justice movements sprung up in every corner of the United States in response to the murders of George Floyd, Breonna Taylor, and dozens of other Black people. There were daily threats of uprooting democracy from a former president that shall not be named, and the surge of anti-Asian hate crime incidents that hit too close to home.

When news of Asian hate crimes popped up on the west coast, I naively convinced myself New York City would be different—that perhaps we are a more tight-knit city that not only learned to coexist but also thrives in the diversity of the multicultural populations—I was wrong. A study by the Center for the Study of Hate and Extremism at California State University, found an 833 percent spike in *documented* incidents of Asian hate crimes even though there was an overall 38 percent decrease in hate crimes in New York City during 2020.

With every breaking news story, my heart sunk deeper and deeper to my stomach. A lady pushed onto the train tracks, a man stabbed on the back with a butcher knife, a grandma set on fire. (Petri & Slotnik, 2021) My mind can't even begin to fathom the pent-up hatred it takes to target our most vulnerable population. A population of grandmas and grandpas who already try to minimize their existence and take up less space in society. Why them?

This is the population who made sacrifices to escape extreme poverty, authoritarian governments, famine, war, and other unfathomable realities to immigrate to the United States. Upon arrival, this population worked unregulated factory jobs so their descendants don't have to even consider it as an option. They built our transcontinental railroad, cooked your beloved Kung Pao chicken, glammed up your nails for your date nights, just to be thanked by xenophobic attacks and scapegoated for the coronavirus pandemic.

In the midst of the pandemic, I found myself fumbling with the plastic packaging of one of the last pepper sprays on the market.

"记住，係咁样揸嘅"—"Remember, hold it like this," I said as I gripped her hand around the canister.

My grandma chuckled as if this was merely a fun role-play. I then looped my finger around the keyring of the personal alarm.

"哦，咩来嚟？有咩用嚟?"—"Oooh, what's that one for?"

I paused. *Fuck. How do you say, "Use this to protect yourself from attackers targeting you based on your age and the color of your skin."*

"用佢来求救"—"Use this to call for help," I replied instead.

I found myself repeating the same cautionary advice my grandma had once told me.

"唔好企 得离地铁咁近啊!"—"Don't stand too close to the train tracks."

"小心啲陌生人啊!"—"Watch out for strangers around you."

"唔好自己一个周围去啊"—"Don't go anywhere alone."

She nodded, shooed me away, and turned her attention back to her daily 8 p.m. TV show.

I glanced over at the pepper spray and the personal alarm sitting idly on the coffee table beside her. The truth was, they were more for my peace of mind than it was for her safety. Knowing how long it takes for her to find her ringing cell phone in her purse, I can only hope that the unspeakable simply doesn't happen in the first place.

Growing up in NYC forces you to live with the fears concerning your safety. But as the years gone by, I learned how to mitigate the risks. If traveling at night or alone, I would sit in the front or middle of the train where the train conductors are within an arm's reach. To prevent theft while napping during my long commute, I would wrap my arms through the straps and wear my backpack on my chest.

While I am a huge proponent of pushing past fears and discomfort, I realized this was a different type of fear. It's not the usual *temporary* fear that electrified us to experience the unknown of a nerve-inducing, diaper-wetting rollercoaster. Instead, this type of fear is more constant—a form of paranoia and anxiety that forces us to be hyper-actively aware of our surroundings. It's terrifying to entertain the thought that my family could become the next Asian hate crime statistic. I could only hope my grandma is more aware of her surroundings while riding the D train, that my mom takes cover if the unthinkable happens at her nail salon.

While there is so much more to say about the hate crimes and the existing internalized racial prejudice in the Asian community, my intention for this book wasn't to instigate and weaponize fear. It's to acknowledge that fear and these issues exist but focus our energy on how we can productively respond to them. I hope we continue to care for and look after our vulnerable populations while encouraging them to speak up about any hate crimes that they have witnessed or experienced. Every documented statistic brings more visibility to a population that has long been rendered invisible. We can continue advocating for mental health resources to those in need, conducting more research on the effects of racial violence on the health and wellbeing of Asian populations, all the while debunking the model minority myth that plagues the Asian community.

We each have our own ways in showing support and doing the hard work. Whether it is having difficult and uncomfortable conversations with our families despite the immigrant transgenerational gap, cultural, and language barriers or whether it is protesting on the streets or donating behind the scenes—there are many ways to "show up" not just one. I hope we can all choose humanity—for the ones we love and for the ones that don't look like us or believe the same things that we do. Choose to speak if even you stutter. Choose hope, even if all that's left is fear.

WHEN IT'S IN THE NAME OF SURVIVAL

As much as I appreciate all New York City has to offer, this organism is bound to encounter system failures.

As a result, I often feel trapped. By trapped, I don't mean working in an unfulfilling nine to five job type of way. Instead, I mean trapped—like a participant in the *Hunger Games* type of way. The arena? None other than the New York City bubble that uses the energy of eight million people's hustle and bustle to fuel the lights of the Empire State Building.

As I was growing up in this city, the mantra was "survival of the fittest." It's instilled in you that your friends are also your enemies and competition. You are starving and experiencing both extreme heat and the cold in the span of seconds, and you are stuck in a jungle you didn't sign up to be in. The only difference is that this game has been going on for more than twenty-two years and the "poisoned berries" are spoiled leftovers that cause food poisoning because I wanted to save money as a broke college student. How do you win this rat race? Easy. Three fool-proof steps:

1. Sabotage your "friends."
2. Land a job at a Fortune 500 company.
3. Finally, get crowned "Best rat employee of the week." Hey, look ma, I made it.

In this city, the people are rewarded for gaining a new skill or adding a new experience on a resume. We overly romanticize enhanced productivity and "burning out" culture. We could even "level up" if you tell others that you are sleep deprived. Because of the saying, "If you can make it here, you can make it anywhere," we are constantly in pursuit of "making it" in New York at the expense of stepping on others and our mental health.

From my experience of being raised in a New York City system, I was indirectly taught that my classmates are our competition and if we want to rise to the top, we will need to have the upper hand. This takes shape in the forms of doing extra credit work, even when I received a 98 percent on a test or putting in more hours at an SAT tutoring session to hopefully have a more appealing score for college board admissions.

Being born and raised in New York has taught me I need to fend for myself and do anything in the name of survival. We are all merely NYC rats, all in pursuit of the end goal of that leftover slice of pizza. Even if it takes jumping subway carts and dodging incoming trains to do so—we will make damn sure we will bring that slice in time for dinner by 8 p.m.

Truth be told, the many years of mental conditioning instilled the need to constantly compete with others. Moreover, I was convinced there was a direct correlation between my productivity and self-worth. In turn, I wrongfully believed my value as a human being would increase if I could market myself as that ideal candidate or student.

"Work smarter, not harder," they would say. "Follow the 80/20 rule," they would also say. All aspects of my life revolved around how I could be more efficient with my time and energy. In college, I discovered Google Calendar, and this changed my life (for the better and for the worse). At first, it was simply a helpful tool to keep track of my classes. Then gradually, I started planning out my day on a more micro scale to maximize my productivity. At times, I would be drowning in immense guilt and regret whenever dinner with friends went two hours off my planned schedule. But one thing led to the next, and I hit rock bottom when I even logged the ten minutes I spent in the bathroom into the calendar. Any time unaccounted for is time spent wasted. That was my mantra.

In addition to juggling the external forces of New York City's toxic productivity culture, there was also the internal pressure as a first child of a Chinese immigrant family household. Whenever I am feeling the immense pressure for an upcoming test or assignment, I would cope by putting my situation in perspective to what my family members had to endure to get me to where I am today.

I would say to myself, "There is a roof over my head, running water, and food in the fridge. You don't have to help Grandma at the textile factories after school, and you certainly don't have to wake up at the crack of dawn to tend the rice patty fields. You are your ancestor's wildest dreams. Why are you complaining about this ten-page paper?"

This "it could be much worse" attitude accumulated into years of stuffing down stress-induced emotions and fears. It took a while before I accepted the fact that although my problems and stressors are not that bad, they are still problems nonetheless. Problems that deserve to be properly addressed and coped with.

I am actively trying to rewire my brain to learn that my self-worth is not dependent on my achievements. My obsession with work is still...well, an obsession, but I'm still walking fast and hopefully making big strides in becoming a better version of myself every day.

The paradox of it all is that regardless of how toxic the New York City culture is for my health, I always run back to my roots. Even if I succeed in escaping this city for a while, no other city in the world could even begin to compare to what New York has to offer. This is especially when I had the privilege of growing up in this city, the hustle inevitably courses through my veins. Yes, the survival rate isn't high, and the competition is cut-throat, but this is exactly why many people do not want to leave. There is nothing more exhilarating and rewarding when you work hard to make the odds work in your favor. This city can make its eight million people feel invincible, alive and in the flesh, and desperate to leverage their powers as mitochondria of the cell.

CHAPTER 9

Wildest Dreams

Dear Mom and Dad,

During the COVID-19 pandemic, we spent a lot of time quarantining together at home before you went back to work. Like *a lot* of time—three months, three weeks, and three days to be exact, but I wasn't really counting. Admittedly, after leaving the nest to live alone in China for a year, moving back into my childhood home wasn't the character development I envisioned. But the silver lining of this pandemic was being able to spend more quality time together as a family.

I honestly don't think I remember the last time we spent so much time together as a family in one place. Mom, you traded your ten-hour workdays to learn how to make 叉烧包—steamed pork buns—from scratch. Dad, you traded your back-to-back business calls to become Mom's sous chef. Your job was to double check if the recipe asked for one tablespoon or one teaspoon. My job was to taste test.

Out of the many things this pandemic has taught me, here are two important ones.

1. We can agree to disagree.

From the fight for social justice to the presidential elections, 2020 really peeled back the layers of so much that is wrong in America. Admittedly, our different upbringings and education backgrounds don't make it easy for us to see eye to eye on certain issues. But I am thankful we are all learning to listen to new perspectives and question the beliefs we once upheld as the truth.

2. We have everything we need to survive.

This pandemic reevaluated my definition of survival. Before this year, survival meant graduating from undergrad with only a handful of breakdowns. It meant speed walking the three blocks home with keys in between my knuckles like Wolverine. It meant cramming for organic chemistry exams and perfecting my hexagon drawings.

But for you and other immigrant families, survival took on another meaning. It meant making ends meet and putting a bowl of rice on the dinner table at the end of the night. It meant working longer days so Derek and I could focus on our schoolwork. It meant facing language barriers, discrimination, and financial uncertainty, but putting a smile on your face for the one hour of family quality time before bedtime.

But when the COVID pandemic hit, the term "survival" shifted again. Survival meant staying alive and healthy. It meant living to experience another day in a safe and warm home. We were all forced to slow down and remember what was important. I'm thankful we were all able to be in each other's presence—to remind ourselves that everything we want, everything we need—we already have it. Because everything boiled down to the bare necessities and having a safe home with Grandma, the both of you, Derek, and of course, Montao, is really all I could ever ask for.

A homebody convert,
Janette

WHEN I'M A FULL-STACK GRANDDAUGHTER

Growing up, my parents worked busy full-time jobs—my father as an IT manager and my mother as a nail technician. It's pretty common in trans-generational Asian households that the grandparents, parents, and kids all live under the same roof. My parents were reluctant to hire some stranger to be the nanny, especially when my grandparents are willing to do it for free.

Does this mean we are...

A. Extremely frugal?
B. Smart with money?

(The answer choice is C: All of the above.)

Hence, my grandma and grandpa were my brother and my primary caretakers throughout elementary and middle school. They had a simple but effective three words vocabulary range that consists of "Hallo, okay, and tank you." This means that despite my broken Cantonese, I had to be full-time on-call translator, interpreter, computer engineer, and other roles that artificial intelligence is slowly taking over. In my grandparent's eyes, I am a computer wizard. But all I do is hold the power button down to restart the device and *poof*. The TV is up and running again in time for their 7 p.m. Beijing Opera.

Despite the additional roles, growing up with grandparents has made me more compassionate, toward others and myself. Throughout the years, they inadvertently taught me it's okay to ask for help and help others—even when things like accepting a friend request on the WeChat app seems self-explanatory. They taught me it's okay to slow down and not allow my to-do list to take control of my day. Sometimes a productive day means doing less of the things that drain energy and more of the things that spark joy, like spending hours tending a backyard garden for spring harvest.

Of course, I didn't make this realization when I slammed doors and rolled my eyes to project my teenage angst. Back then, as a typical young and naïve child who just wanted to go to the mall with her friends, I was frustrated with my grandparents' language impediment. Regrettably, it even seemed like a major source of inconvenience and embarrassment. This clouded judgment made me neglect the fact that my parents and grandparents have risked it all to come to a foreign country that predominantly speaks a language they don't know but three words—all in the hope of a better life for themselves and their progeny. Hell, I wouldn't be sitting here typing a book in *English* if it weren't for their valor, hard work, and survival skills, so I owe it all to them.

WHEN I'M 8,062 MILES AWAY FROM HOME

Eight times out of ten, I can hear the distinct voice of some Asian grandma yelling Gui Ling Gao after I step off the D train at Grand Street station.

If I didn't understand Cantonese or Taishanese, I would've mistaken her yelling for a wolf cry for help.

But no, this sweet grandma was just employing her number one marketing tactic to sell 龟苓膏 (Gui Ling Gao)—tortoise herbal jelly on the crowded streets of Chinatown, Manhattan.

Like my parents, this Chinese grandma most likely belonged to the mass exodus of families who immigrated from Taishan, China to New York City. Back in the 1980s, my parents fled their hometowns in pursuit of a better life in the United States. They heard stories about the American dream, the freedom, and the potential for great success, so they took a leap of faith.

While others relocated to major port cities like San Francisco and Toronto, my family, along with other Taishanese families, chose to settle down in Chinatown, New York City. My grandma and aunt started out sewing garments in textile factories in the Lower East Side, while my dad went to Seward Park High School and worked part time as a waiter in Chinese restaurants.

To my parents, their sole priority was and still is survival.

As I was growing up, I was constantly reminded of my parents' and their families' humble beginnings. This reminder manifested itself as childhood stories and threats about the potential consequences of not eating every grain of rice in the bowl. (I was told that every leftover grain of uneaten rice reincarnated itself into a new pimple on my face—to which my prepubescent body-conscious self-proceeded to lick the bowl sparkling clean.)

I've heard little bits and chunks of stories from my parents' childhood. We would watch a Chinese movie with a setting in rural China and my mom would point at the TV and say:

"我哋以前嘅乡下就係咁样噶!"—"Back in the day, our villages looked just like that!"

"揾日带你同Derek去睇下我哋以前係点生活嘅"—"One day we will bring you and Derek to show you how we lived back then," my dad added.

I would look up from my phone at the TV screen and nod. I mentally filed the movie scene into the brain archives of my parents' childhood home under the "Poor and Broke" category.

Finally, in the summer of 2018, my preconceptions of their childhood upbringings were confirmed when we took a family trip to Taishan, China. This was my first time traveling to my parents' hometown and just my third time in China itself.

My parents grew up in the rural area of Taishan, a small city located in the Guangdong province in southeast China. More specifically, my dad's family is from 冲蒌镇 (the town of Chong Lou), and my mom's family is from 白沙镇 (the town of BaiSha).

Their villages are so remote that the only way to locate them are going down a dirt road path for fifteen minutes, making a right at an electrical pole, then driving for ten more minutes until you see *the tree*. Then from there, it is only a couple hundred yards until you pass the pile of rubble at the entrance of their town.

When we arrived, my dad wrestled with the rusty lock that guarded the front entrance. A few moments later, we heard a *click,* and he nudged the doors open. The wooden door creaked, welcoming the original owner, three decades after he said 再见—goodbye. This was the same wooden door that made cameos in my dad's childhood stories. In his lectures about safety, he would mention how he had to use a broomstick to block the door as a form of home security.

The house smelled exactly like how one would expect an abandoned home to smell: stale and musky. The overcast sky was at the verge of rainfall that day. But that didn't stop some daylight from sneaking into the home through the shattered windows. At the front door, I was confronted with high ceilings and two wooden staircases that led up to the second and third floor. The one that led up the third floor collapsed halfway, leaving a gaping hole and overhanging nails in its place.

At first glance, the house looked large—almost the same size as the home we have in Brooklyn. But a closer look revealed the cracked walls, neglected furniture, and exposed brick walls stained from natural erosion. I thought back to my recent internet search history for faux brick wallpaper.

I stood at the home entrance, awkwardly shifting my weight on the concrete floor below me. Below me, there were pieces of broken glass, wired hangers, wooden chips, chipped paint, among other rubble that had accumulated for the past thirty years. I sidestepped them as best as I could; No one gave me the memo to wear sneakers instead of open-toed sandals that day.

My parents began to set up the table of offerings for the ancestors. A cooked chicken, a slab of pork, snacks, and cups of white wine. I wondered about the last time an offering was made in this home. As I ventured around the home, the familiar scent of burning incense lingered in to fill the vacancy of every room.

Slowly and cautiously, I climbed the steps to one of the rooms on the second floor. I tucked my hands to my side, careful not to disturb an important artifact in the fear that I would anger the spirits that lived in the home. Above me, there hung a bare light bulb dangling from a wire from the ceiling. It reminded me of the Edison "vintage" style light-bulb that hung in my own room.

In the room, there were leftover pieces of wooden planks, empty glass bottles, woven baskets and other items that once served a purpose—all coated in decades worth of dust.

Dad found his way into the room and placed his hands on his hips. He did a 360-degree scan of the room and suddenly picked up an antiquated ceramic jug with a smile on his face. I could've sworn I saw a similar-looking jug at the Metropolitan Museum of Art.

"你知唔知, 我哋以前就係用依啲装米噶。"—"You know, we use to store rice in these," he said, gesturing the jug toward me.

I nodded. "Why not clean this place up?" I asked, shielding my nose from the floating dust bunnies. "At least repair the broken windows?"

He sighed and said, “冇用嘅, 啲贼以后都係会来偷嘢嘅啦!”—“No point in doing so; the house will just get broken into again by thieves.”

And that was the only thing I remember my dad saying to me about the house that day as he walked around his childhood home.

That day, my brother and I also visited my mom’s childhood home in a nearby village. Her home had the same naked lightbulb on a string, wooden planks for bed frames, and a DIY broomstick made with stray tree branches bounded together with red strings. They casually walked around their former homes, occasionally pointed out an old artifact, but said nothing more.

I thought about our current Brooklyn home—the recessed ceiling lights, the running tap water, and the Dyson vacuum sitting in our closet. I wondered how it must have felt for my parents, whether coming back to their childhood homes made them feel like they had lived here in a past life. I wondered how it felt to know that food is now guaranteed at a local neighborhood supermarket, rather than relying on an unpredictable harvest. I wondered what it felt to be driven by the survival mentality, a mindset that enabled them to not just survive but thrive in the states.

In my mom’s old bedroom, I stared into the cracked heart-shaped mirror on her wooden dresser. Even with the old stickers residue and debris collected from decades ago, I could still make out a dusty reflection of myself. It was then that I realized my parents brought me all the way—8,062 miles away from our home in Brooklyn—not just to show me how *they* have lived back then. But to show me where *I could’ve* grown up, had they not taken that leap of faith to immigrate to New York City.

WHEN IN THE PURSUIT OF PURPOSE

A couple of months into 2020, I came upon Bo Ren's tweet:

"My parents were tasked with the job of survival and I with self-actualization. The immigrant generational gap is real. What a luxury it is to search for purpose, meaning, and fulfillment." (@Bosefina, 2017)

After reading this quote, I gained a greater sense of clarity, as if the author were sub-tweeting me.

I didn't realize the extent to which the immigrant trans-generational gap has influenced mine and my parents' perceptions on many topics and issues. This divide between my generation and my parents' generation is typically summarized in the sentence, "They will never understand the problems that we have to face today."

But in truth, the reality of the situation is exactly the opposite. If I got cast in the movie about my parents' survival story, I would get killed off faster than Shonda Rhimes killing off another one of the main leads on *Grey's Anatomy.*

I used to think that luxury manifested itself into the form of material possessions. For instance, owning a mansion, driving a fancy car, buying another Louis Vuitton bag in Europe, or maybe if I was feeling especially frivolous, agreeing to get extra guacamole with my Chipotle order. But now, I realized just how subjective that term is. To my parents, "luxuries" meant having a side dish of meat at the dinner table. It meant having a centralized indoor heating. It meant receiving an education.

I recognize that I even have the luxury of facing first-world "problems."

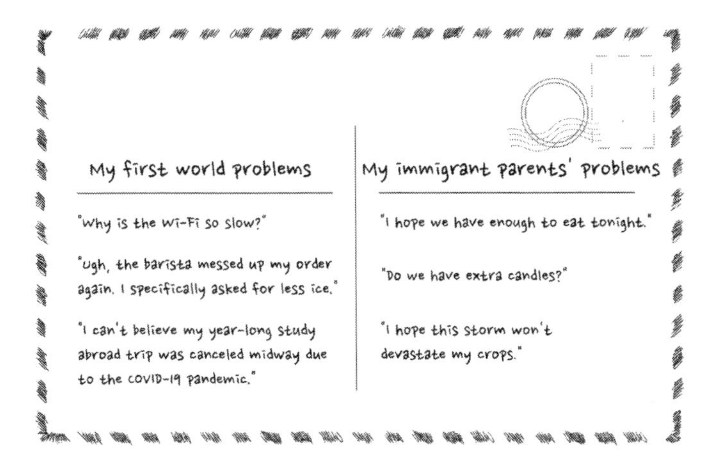

The more I become self-aware of this topic, the more I realize how we all have it wrong. Luxuries are not tangible. For me, "luxuries" reveal themselves in the form of having free time, getting eight hours of sleep, getting to spend quality time with family and friends, and most recently, the ability to be self-aware of my purpose in life.

This quote forced me to sit down, process, and reevaluate this "p word" that has been haunting me for several years now. *Purpose.*

For years, I've felt torn in between this dichotomy between purpose versus profit. My parents have willingly taken on the burden of the *survival mentality* so I wouldn't have to worry about my next meal or whether or not I have to choose between getting a free education or working in the rice patty fields. But now, I am confronted with the "first world" problems of searching for a greater purpose, the meaning of life, and how this empty jar inside of me can be fulfilled with joy and meaning.

I have the luxury of worrying about the current and future state of the world from the climate crisis to the future state of the nation given the possibility of another term with a divisive president. I am worried about our basic human right to health care and how just one hundred fossil fuel producers are responsible for over 70 percent of greenhouse gas emissions. I am worried about women's reproductive rights and how they are ironically governed by conservative white men who get off at the thought of controlling women's bodies.

But to my parents, and many others in their generation, the act of worrying can't put food on the table. Finding my purpose can't pay the water and electricity bills. Settling for a low paying yet fulfilling job can't keep the roof above our heads.

But to myself and perhaps others fortunate enough to be born in the midst of the Gen Z and Millennial generation, we are at least willing to take that leap of faith while remaining grateful for those who laid the foundation for us. I don't believe I have to choose between purpose or profit. I want my values to not only align with my occupation but also drive me to fulfill a higher purpose in life. I want to be part of the frontier tackling the many social issues and global crises that our planet faces at the moment.

I don't believe being more self-aware is necessarily a bad thing either. By being more self-aware, I am more conscious of how one person can make a difference. I believe that my purpose and desire to generate social impact shouldn't have to be compromised in favor of buying a mansion or a fancy car.

To quote a billboard I saw while driving across the Manhattan Bridge, "I am my ancestors' wildest dreams." When I saw this, I immediately recorded the quote in the Notes app of my phone. So that whenever I need to jot down a quick grocery list or find that Wi-Fi password that looks like a toddler had chosen by slamming a keyboard, I am reminded of this affirmation. I am reminded of my parents' decision to immigrate and how their children can dare to dream. I am reminded that my parents didn't come all this way to let dreams just be dreams.

TIME CAPSULE IV

Read This for a Dose of Nostalgia

CHAPTER 10

The Summers That Got Away

Dear Mom and Dad,

Remember that time I fell and bumped my head trying to take down the shower head when I was eight years old?

Mom, you weren't home, but Dad and Derek were. I remember feeling so "grown" that I could now shower on my own. This was one of the first steps in me becoming a *woman* and I was excited I could perform all the Disney classics in the shower. That night, even before I got my pajamas from my room, I climbed onto the edge of the tub and tippy toed to take down the showerhead. The next thing I knew, I woke up at the bottom of the tub with a throbbing headache and blurry vision.

Dad, you probably heard the loud thump from the kitchen. I heard you call out my name, and I screamed back, "I'M OKAY, I JUST FELL IN THE SHOWER," but there was audibly no sound coming out of my mouth. I tried screaming again for you but again, I was left mouthing the words that I wanted to say.

When you found me, you carried me into the living room and told Derek to call 911. I tried to explain by saying, "I AM FINE, DAD," but again, nothing was coming out of my mouth. After a while, I thankfully regained my ability to speak again. Dad, remember when you told Derek to grab all the cereal boxes and forced me to read the labels.

"Whole grain wheat, sugar, rice flour, canola oil, fructose, malto...dex...trin? Dex...tro...se? Salt, cinnamon, tri...sodium pho...sph...ate?"

I was reading ingredients I didn't know how to pronounce, and Dad, you mistook that as a symptom of the possible concussion.

Mom and Dad, I never told you this but after I woke up in the bathtub, my first thought wasn't "Oh no! I can never speak again" or "I am so scared that I might have some traumatic brain injury."

Instead, my first and immediate thought was, *Yes! That means no Saturday school tomorrow. I won't have to take the spelling test that I haven't begun studying for yet.*

I could imagine how traumatic and terrified you must have been when you discovered that your daughter suddenly could not speak anymore. It is nowhere near the same level or trauma you experienced, but trust me, I am also scarred for life after years of enduring Saturday school, summer school, SHSAT prep and SAT prep. Have I told you about those stories from my elementary school days?

Your now very talkative daughter,
Janette

WHEN IT'S THE EFFORT THAT COUNTS

Anyone who watched Disney Channel as a kid should know about the movie *The Parent Trap* directed by Nancy Meyers.

To this day, this is my favorite movie of all time (the 1998 version—not the 1961 version). The movie is about two eleven-year-old twin girls (both played by the iconic Lindsay Lohan) separated at birth due to their parents' divorce. But they were reunited when they ended up at the same summer camp. After their reunion, they made a pact to exchange places in order to spend time with the other parent. After they reveal their true selves, their parents are forced to see each other again, hoping this reunion could rekindle their love for one another.

For a while, after I first watched the movie, I was obsessed with the idea I had a twin living on the other side of the world. Like in the movie, I learned how to play (Chinese) poker and practiced fencing with a broomstick at home to prepare for the possibility that I would have to challenge my twin in a duel.

But little did I know that the most unrealistic aspect of this fantasy wasn't the possibility of having a biological twin. Nor was it the possibility of becoming an expert at poker or fencing. Instead, the most unrealistic aspect of it would be trapping my parents into agreeing to send me off to summer *camp* rather than summer *school.*

On the night of the ask, I said *please please please please please* so many times it didn't even sound like an actual word anymore.

In response, my parents laughed and said:

"你想成个暑假都出去玩，仲要我畀钱"—"You want to play all summer? And you want me to pay someone to watch you play?"

"I won't *play* all the time in summer camp, Mom. I will be doing scavenger hunts, arts and crafts, zip-lining...I will also *learn* how to kayak and *learn* how to make friendship bracelets. It's a lot of *learning* not *playing*. Doesn't that sound like fun?" I whined.

I enunciated the capital L in the word "learn" in case she didn't hear it the first three times I've said it.

"FUN? 你知学习够FUN啦, 读书都好FUN啊, 做功课都特别FUN啊!"—"Fun? You know studying is also fun, reading is also fun, doing homework is especially fun!"

"But..."

"冇but, 你一定要返暑期补习班!"—"No buts, you have to take summer classes."

I knew my chances of successfully trapping my parents to send me off to summer camp were pretty slim. They also prepaid the tuition months beforehand, so it was futile efforts. But, hey, I tried right?

Parents: 1, Janette: 0.

WHEN LIFE WAS SIMPLE AND STRESS-FREE

Spending two additional months in school wasn't part of my Pinterest vision board for the perfect summer vacation.

I had imagined waking up naturally at 2 p.m., knocking on my neighbor's door to ask if she can come outside to play, riding bikes, and playing freeze-tag. By the time the sun sets, I would come home and gulp down a gallon of ice-cold tap water before planting myself on the couch with a Pop-Ice frozen popsicle in hand just in time to watch a rerun episode of *That's So Raven*. Life would be simple and stress-free.

Instead, I had to wake up at 8 a.m. to the sound of my parents banging pots and pans together. Before heading out the door, I quickly took a bite out of the hot dog bao.

Just like my relationship with my sibling and NYC in the winter, I had a love-hate relationship with summer school.

On one hand, I accepted my fate that I will never experience a "summer vacation" like the rest of our non-Asian peers. It was still torturous to try to pass it off as a "fun thing" to do.

I arrived on the first day of fall classes, dreading the "How was your summer?" conversation. I anxiously took a seat in the lunchroom next to some of my non-ABC friends who were, right on cue, eagerly asking one another about the highlights of their summer.

"I spent the whole summer in Florida with my grandparents, we went to Disney like every week!"

"I went to summer camp, and we did arts and crafts, made s'mores around the campfire...and look!

She stuck out her wrist and showed off her new arm candy.

"We even learned how to make friendship bracelets!" she continued, even though nobody asked.

"See, this chevron one is with Emma, this one is with Katelyn S. from California, this one is with Catelin W. from Texas, and this one..."

I grabbed the invisible magic speaking conch and interrupted. "Well, I went to summer school." It sounded more like a brag than I intended. Even I couldn't convince myself to make it sound like summer school was better than Disney World or summer camp.

Everyone around me gasped as if I had just offended their mothers.

The Florida girl lowered her voice and whispered, "Did you...did you get left back from school?"

"NO! OF COURSE NOT!" I exclaimed.

It was now my turn to be offended that she could say such a thing to me—an obedient, always eager to please, the eldest female child of a Chinese household. My grandma prayed too often to the god of education for me to get left back.

I continued to say, "My parents just want me to get ahead in next year's material and make sure that I don't forget everything I learned last year. That's all."

"Wow...but summer school must suck when you are supposed to be on break," said Caitlyn Z. as she twiddled with her friendship bracelets.

"You have no idea...," I sighed.

WHEN THE KNOCK-OFF IS JUST AS GOOD

Despite not being able to live out my inner white-girl-at-summer-camp fantasies, I didn't entirely *hate* summer school either. The silver lining was when I got to see some of my friends again after a week-long hiatus.

For as long as I could remember, every summer consisted of going to summer school, usually with the same Cabbage Patch Kids of Asian friends at school. In these summer schools, 99.99 percent of my classmates were also ABCs (American Born Chinese). Even though none of us willingly enlisted to attend this summer school boot camp, we were all connected somehow. We shared the common grounds of having strict tiger parents along with a synchronous, pulsating desire to make them proud.

Before the first day of classes, all the students had to take a diagnostic test to determine which class we would test into—A or B class—with A being the "smart" class and B being the "*less*-smart" class. Even though the class separation was never explicitly explained, it doesn't take an Einstein genius, let alone a fifth grader, to differentiate between the two.

The school could've named the class *ketchup* and *mustard*, but the kids would've figured it out by seeing where the consistently smart kids ended up. In my opinion, these kids didn't even need prep. But their parents needed a babysitter for two months. These kids merely skewed the class average to the right, wrecking my chances with being okay with a 90 percent grade. But it's not their fault that they were born gifted and talented.

No one admitted it, but everyone wanted a spot in the A class. Even after a day in summer school, everyone would know that the A class was less of a "nerds only" thing and more of a form of social status. "A" class was like the Rolex of watches, the Tesla of cars, and the Charmin of three-ply toilet paper.

Hence, on the diagnostic test day of summer school, getting into the A class was flagged as a top priority—partially because this would determine whether or not I get to see my friends for the next seven weeks and partially because I know that I would let my parents down if I tested into the B class.

When the results were announced, I felt a wave of relief knowing I avoided the house slipper beating from my parents for yet another summer. And more importantly, my friends were by my side. After school, we spent the long summer nights dancing to Katy Perry's 2010 summer anthem, "California Gurls." We were a couple of East Coast preteen girls belting a west coast song with lyrics we didn't understand. As we ate Pop-Ice until our tongues turned Smurf blue, we hovered over the air conditioning unit and laughed about how the blast of cool air would form a baby belly with our shirts.

"Ah, just like a knock off low-budget summer camp," I would say to my friends.

WHEN THE ENDS MIGHT JUSTIFY THE MEANS

In retrospect, I realized how fucked up it was to be a guinea pig within the A/B class system divide. I remember focusing so much of my energy on getting into the "A" class because that was where all the *smart* kids belong. The smart kids were constantly told that they were not only *gifted and talented*, but they also have the potential to be *Harvard* material. There was a huge emphasis on grades in order to *get ahead*. I knew this. My teachers knew this. And my parents especially knew this because they kept sending me back to run on the hamster wheel every summer.

As a result, when these "A" students suddenly get a "B" or even worse, don't get into Harvard, they are left questioning their existence. We have been told our whole lives that we are born *gifted and talented*, capable of manifesting success at every hidden corner. But when we encounter failures or when expectations are not met, we are left gasping for air amid a sea of other high-functioning, hopeless overachievers.

This is why after years of shuffling through what I call the 4S System (summer school, Saturday school, SHSAT prep and SAT prep), it is inevitable that I learned to associate grades and academic achievement with my self-worth. I learned to associate the letter "A" by receiving positive feedback and affirmations from teachers and parents. I learned that to *get ahead* I have to continue striving for the "best of the best" and the highest expectations. But if I fell short and ended up in only "above average," I perceived it as moments of failure and ineptitude.

It wasn't until I've grew out of the 4S system that I learned about the term "imposter syndrome." Imposter syndrome describes feeling insecure in one's ability or achievements. It is manifested into the fear of never being "good enough," "knowledgeable enough," or "smart enough" in comparison to my peers around me. It is also the anxiety and fear of being called out for being a fraud by superiors or authority figures.

This form of academic conditioning was encouraged because it wasn't customary for me to celebrate successes because that was what I was supposed to be doing anyway. How would I know how to overcome failure when I was only taught to celebrate successes? On the other end of the spectrum, failures are more often brought up, weaponized as reminders while disguising itself as words of encouragement. Although these failures were never brought up explicitly, they weighed heavily on me. I wince at the thought that despite being handed all this extra academic support, my parents' money was flushed down the drain.

This term essentially summed up the years of detrimental effects from academic conditioning that manifested itself into other parts of my life.

As I am writing this, it pains me to admit how often and quickly I try to talk myself out of something even before I begin. This is the conversation I had with myself before I published my book campaign.

Admittedly, I'm aware that all of this smack talk about imposter syndrome, prep schools, tutoring sessions, and even having the time to write a book all come from a place of privilege. I was fortunate my parents were able to financially support this extra academic help.

But at the same time, it's important to acknowledge the shortcomings of a glorified meritocratic system and the consequences associated with imposter syndrome. This syndrome programmed years of feeling like I am not doing enough in pursuit of my academic, career, or personal goals. It made me question the validity of receiving a scholarship or a good test grade. It even made me associate my peer's successes as an equivalence to my failures. With the root of the problem stemming from years of insecurity, it will take years of unlearning and rewiring of the brain before I can hopefully accept that self-worth comes from within ourselves, rather than external sources.

So, do the ends justify the means? It depends on who you're asking.

To my immigrant parents? Probably yes.

With their Chinese cultural background, education was a path to success and usually, that path to success is synonymous with getting good grades. They were also jaded and unaware of fostering the holistic attributes of a college candidate. Extracurriculars. Leadership experience. Community service. The whole shebang. It would be wrong of me to blame them for all of my character flaws when to them, education in itself was deemed as a privilege in their home country.

But to my adolescent insecure self who just wanted to go to summer camp—probably not.

CHAPTER 11

When Blood is Thicker than Water

Dear Derek,

First of all, I want this on record that I am Mom and Dad's favorite child. Now that the important stuff is said and done, there are a couple of other things I also want to address.

1. You do a really half-ass job at washing the dishes. You have to wash the front and *back* side of the plate as well as pick out all the nasty shit from the drain. Both are included in the job description. Speaking of which, it's your turn to do them.
2. There is no reason why you need to take hour-long showers. Please be considerate that you have three other family roommates in this house who also need to use the communal bathroom.
3. Keep in mind that I am our dog Montao's third favorite, right after mom and dad. He would tell me this every time I take him out for a walk.

4. Thanks for fueling my competitive spirit and teaching me how to cope with the duality of being a sore winner and loser. You don't suck as much as you used to.

Your favorite and only sister,
Janette

WHEN I SIGNED UP FOR A LIFELONG INTERNSHIP

One time, when I was eight years old, I chased my younger brother around the house with a butcher knife.

Do I remember why I did it?

Nope.

Was I aware of the dangers and safety precautions of handling a sharp object?

Nope again—didn't even cross my mind.

But did I have fun watching him run around the house screaming in snot and tears?

You bet I did.

In my defense, he probably did something so utterly repulsive and infuriating to provoke me to grab the knife from the kitchen cabinet. It was somewhere along the lines of using his new toy, the Nerf machine gun, to set the target right at the space between my eyes. Or perhaps it was intentionally launching a giant rubber ball on my head to test the bounciness for a "science experiment." In other words, we didn't get along most of the times.

I am almost exactly two years older than Derek. We are both May babies, but he was born a Taurus while I was born a Gemini. Tauruses are earth signs known to be more introverted and creatures of habit while Geminis are air signs who are adaptable and social creatures. For as long as I could remember, my brother and I operated on different frequencies. He's stubborn, hot-tempered, and loved physically taxing sports while I was sarcastic, impulsive, and loved taking mid-day naps. My younger brother, Derek, was no saint, and he knew it too when he infamously threw a chair at his kindergarten teacher.

Most preschoolers would kick, scream and cry (in no particular order) at the thought of their parents abandoning them in a strange building with other kicking, screaming and crying children. But Derek learned early that actions speak louder than words—hence, the chair-throwing incident.

In response, my parents decided that the best way to appease his violent nature was to send him to karate classes. Sounds counterintuitive, I know.

I remember participating in his first karate "test trial" training session. It was supposed to be a one-on-one session with an instructor, but my mom dragged me into it. I wouldn't have gone if it weren't for the fact that she was my ride home.

That day, after a karate class ended and a bunch of pre-pubescent boys in white robes filed out, my brother and I were summoned onto the sweaty mat. I stood awkwardly, shifting my feet back and forth, and letting my arms hang by my side like two sausages. A couple of feet to my left, my brother had already gotten into a fighter's stance with closed fists. I knew he was imitating the stance that he saw on an episode of *Power Rangers*, thirty minutes beforehand.

The instructor praised my brother for his strong form and instructed us to hold our fists up in the air in front of our faces.

"Nice form, Derek!" said the instructor.

He continued and demonstrated, "Now hold your fists up like this to protect your face."

Derek obliged.

I looked over to my left and suddenly noticed the serious look on Derek's face. He had his left leg in and right foot out. If it weren't for his uncharacteristically calm demeanor, I would have assumed he was doing the hokey pokey. His stance looked strong and unshakable. His hands clenched and awaited instructions for his next strike.

I, on the other hand, also held my now sweaty fists up in the air. But unlike Derek, I look like I just got caught stealing a handful of M&Ms at the fifth grade Halloween dance in the school's lunchroom.

"Now let me get a HI-YA and a left jab!" screamed the instructor.

Derek bellowed out a "HI YAAA" and struck the air with a swift left jab.

I managed to let out a squeak. "Hey ya."

In the years following, I dutifully took up my role as a human punching bag and took an unpaid internship as an experimental rat for Derek's practice triangle holds. The goal was for Derek to learn how to channel his anger and emotions in a constructive manner through these karate classes, and the funny thing was it worked. He trained for years in MMA (mixed martial arts) classes, won numerous competitions, granted my parents bragging privileges, and six years later, he rightfully claimed his black belt title.

As for me, the closest I've gone to participating in sports is when I form a football goal post with my fingers to differentiate between my left and right. Admittingly, my brother is better than me at many things. Whether it is sports, SAT math, or SAT math problems about sports, he always managed to do the opposite of leveling out the playing field. While he may had dominated the physical realm of sports, my forte lied in the virtual worlds of Nintendo DS. Unlike the real world, go karting in the world of Mario Kart also doesn't discriminate against female drivers. And if he disagreed, then we chose to settle things in the virtual world.

WHEN WE RELIED ON OUR SIXTH SENSE

Around the first decade of the 2000s, the Nintendo DS was a statement piece. This Japanese device was equivalent to a modern-day 2020 flexing of an Apple Watch. My red and black DS was my baby and at eight years old, I was her proud single mother.

When we were both in elementary school, my brother and I would wrap up the day with nightly game sessions on our Nintendo DS. We would alternate in playing racing games in Mario Kart and mini games in Super Mario Party, or watch one another beat Bowser in Super Mario Bros.

On most occasions, Super Mario Party would be our top choice even after my parents had already called for lights out. We performed this routine so many times that we not only could hear incoming footsteps, but we could predict which parent was coming in to check on us based on the cadence of their footsteps. My dad's footsteps are heavy as he drags one foot behind the other. My mom's footsteps are light and swift, like the motion she uses to hit us with her slipper and/or hanger when we misbehaved.

When our sixth sense detected we are currently in the "danger zone," we would quickly slam our DS shut, slip it underneath our pillows, and shut our eyes right before Mom or Dad cracked open the door to check on us. When the coast was clear, Derek and I would waste no time and continue the suspenseful mini games.

In moments like this, I remember feeling grateful to have Derek next to me. A younger brother who agreed to trick our parents and fake sleep just so we could stealthily play our DS in the middle of the night. I would think to myself, perhaps this round-headed little brother could become my best friend. By day, we could race up and down our block on bicycles and by night, we could put our minds together and defeat the big boss and the other NPCs (non-player characters). He was the Luigi to my Mario and for a second—just a second—I forgot what it's like for him to get on my nerves.

That is until he would firmly decide that "I've cheated" and would proceed to yank the game chip from the device. Hence, terminating the game along with my false reality that we could get along without arguments. If it weren't for the fact that we were hiding from our mother, and by definition, the wrath of her slipper, that act would've triggered the cycle of the screaming, kicking, and pinching all over again.

WHEN TO ADDRESS THE ELEPHANT IN THE ROOM

On the topic of the sibling dynamic in a traditional Chinese household, it would be unjustified, and even offensive, if I don't address the elephant in the room: double standards.

So, when the elephant answers nature's calling, you can already guess who has to pick up the dung.

Some days, my grandma came upstairs and helped us tidy up the house. As my grandma wrung out the water from a rag, I saw her glance over at me from my peripheral vision. I don't budge.

"你係时候要拾下依度啦!"—"You got to start doing some housework around here," my grandma said as she wipes off the layer of dust on the shelves.

I've never heard her repeat that sentence to my younger brother.

"唔好整日出街啦, 留低喺屋企"—"Don't go out so much; stay home instead," she would say as my brother leaves the house to hang out with his friends.

"天黑前要返到屋企啊"—"Come home before it gets dark outside," she would say when just the night before, my brother came home at 1 a.m.

Admittedly, this is cautionary advice spoken from a place of love. Yet it would be delusional to pretend that gender roles are not baked into the equation. Back in my grandmother's day, gender stereotypes were heavily enforced, especially in the villages. Women oversaw cooking, cleaning, and working in the fields and men had to work in construction. But nowadays, everyone must pull their weight. If we are to move forward toward a more gender-equality centered society, it's important to raise children with the same standards.

I have a theory that girls, especially daughters in Chinese households, are so good at picking up other people's slack whether it is in the workplace or a "group" project. This is because they've already been conditioned at home. Similarly, I am expected to do house chores like wash the dishes, do the laundry, mop the floors. But when I pull the "What about Derek?" card, I get slapped in the face with his "Get out of jail free card" because as my mother would say, "He has a lot of homework."

~~Bull~~ Elephant shit.

WHEN DISCIPLINE HITS DIFFERENTLY IN AN IMMIGRANT HOUSEHOLD

Over the years, I learned that growing up with a sibling, especially a younger sibling of the opposite sex, is its own type of psychological thriller.

Unreliable narrators

Elements of fear and terror

- [x] A greater understanding of what makes each other tick

As I grow older, I learned that other siblings would not make the same analogy. Therefore, I am always simultaneously surprised and impressed whenever I hear testimonies about how my friends and their siblings get along well together. For some of them, they are also each other's best friends—which I call absolute bullshit, but hey, who am I to judge?

I would interrogate my friends and ask: "So you and your siblings like *actually* get along? No fights? No scars? No bite marks? Nothing?"

To which my friends would give a nonchalant reply: "Nope, not really, we would get into small disagreements here and there but nothing crazy."

"Bull...I mean, *but*...what about full-blown arguments that your parents had to end by spanking the *both* of you?" I pestered.

My mind flashed back to the tingling red burn that left more of an emotional scar than a physical scar on my left leg. Whenever Derek and I get into petty arguments about the TV remote or the Nintendo DS, our mom would watch silently from the sidelines. As she folded the week's laundry, she would occasionally turn her attention away from the TVB Chinese dramas to glare at us. And if we were still screaming after she matched the last pair of socks, she would decide that after her ten and a half hours workday, enough was enough.

Mom wouldn't even give us a warning.

All we heard was the forced opening of the closet door, the light but quick footsteps coming down the hallway, and the next thing we knew, Derek and I were running to the other end of the house, climbing on top of the bed.

With our backs against the wall, we were hoping that the thick winter blankets could shelter us from the swift hits of the plastic hanger. Even then, Mom would rip off our *blanket shield* and ignore the stream of tears, mucus and everything in between bursting from our faces.

We were now kicking our legs in all directions, the equivalence of running in zigzag formation so that the armed gunman has a lower chance of striking you. My mom never missed.

I braced myself for the impact.

Swift Smack.

My brother clamped his right leg and winced in pain.

Swift Smack.

I retreated my legs to my chest and cried out in anguish.

No preferential treatment here.

Mom waved the weapon in the air and threatened us again. "你哋仲打唔打?"—"Are you both still going to hit each other?"

Derek and I shook our head in unison and my mom left the room just as quickly as she came in, returning the weapon to its rightful home in the coat closet.

"Nope," my friend said, snapping me back into reality.

"*But*, what about fighting over the TV remote when you wanted to watch *The Wizards of Waverly Place* but he wanted to watch *The Suite Life of Zack and Cody*? You *must* have fought over the TV at some point, right?"

"I mean there was one time...nope, we talked it out and agreed to watch *Kim Possible* instead together."

"Unbelievable...," I would reply as I studiously take mental notes.

Every time, I would be dumbfounded and unconvinced of their responses. When I was younger, I believed there must've been some magic-sibling-harmony-herbal tea that my parents didn't feed to me and my brother. While I often wanted to accidentally put a pillow over his face while he slept, there were still a handful of instances that reminded me how we got along.

WHEN WE ARE STRONGER UNITED

Growing up with a sibling forces you to learn all sorts of necessary life skills from a young age.

1. Arguing over the TV remote? → The art of negotiation
2. Wrestling over a shared toy? → The art of self defense
3. Sharing the last scoop of ice cream? → The art of sharing the last scoop of ice cream

As the years went by, we argued and wrestled (less) over the last scoop of ice cream. But especially in the later years of my high school and college years, I found myself maturing into the big sister role that I was born in.

As I grew more self-aware and learned to navigate the "real world," I wanted to instill some life skills that I've accumulated over the years. So, in the traditional old-fashioned way of communication in the culture of my household, I tried to express my love and guidance through acts of service.

To me, this meant preventing my younger brother from falling victim to the bureaucracies of the college application system. From my experience, navigating the college application process in an immigrant household is its own type of Iron Man Triathlon. In my high school, I graduated with a class of over 1,000 seniors. And all 1,000 of us clueless airheads had the mere help of *two* college guidance counselors. It was stressful. It was exhausting. At seventeen years old, I even started growing gold hair in addition to my white hair. I didn't know I could unlock that premium feature of myself so soon.

Since I've been through the journey myself, I didn't want Derek to suffer (as much) as I did. Regardless, he still had to run the race, but the least I could do is to show him where to follow the mile markers.

When I had to cram for my Advanced Placement coursework in high school, I would try to pass down study hacks that I've learned. When he was applying for colleges, I would offer to read over his personal statement essays and drop little nuggets of advice, hoping that he would pick it up. When he was applying for internships, I would try to stress the message that proactivity and persistence get better results than being a sitting duck.

I'd realize that as the years go by, you'd see your sibling as less of a roommate who you have to coexist with and more of a lifeline. One who has witnessed each other's bed-wetting stage and tolerated the atomic farts, but still willing to pick up your one phone call from the police station. There is also nobody, not even a therapist, who is able to understand the intricacies of the family dynamic better than your sibling.

Over the years, we both learned the unique mannerisms of our family members. We learned how to tell when someone is in a good mood and when to avoid eye contact with them for the rest of the night. We learned that while blood is thicker the water, a family feud could easily turn cousins into strangers. We learned how to build forts with dining room chairs and weatherproof it by draping it with heavy winter blankets. We even learned to memorize the spots on the floorboards that creaked the loudest at night.

On those nights, we intentionally stayed up past 2 a.m. to wait for the mother cockroach to come out of hiding.

"Janette, it's back," he whispered from across the silence of the living room. Immediately, we assumed our predetermined positions and got ready for attack.

I stood on the edge of a chair and waved my mom's slipper in the air. The first time I witnessed this trojan roach, I was stunned. She was even bigger than how my brother had described to me. It looked like a costume that a thousand smaller roaches were using as a tactical shield. The first couple of times, we hesitated, and the roach escaped underneath the crack of the radiator. But not this time, the slipper never missed.

This time, she resurfaced and strutted across the creaky hardwood floors. She was confident, audacious, and resilient—everything I aspired to be.

But this time, Derek and I came prepared on the front lines. In a coordinated attack, Derek neutralized the beast with the cinnamon apple air freshener, and I swept in with the slipper for the final blow.

Immediately, we turned our heads toward the direction of our parents' room. *Silence.* We were in the clear. A few moments later, we turned our attention back to the crime scene, then at each other.

I swiftly touched my nose with my pointer finger. "Not it," I whispered. "Clean it up bitch."

It is in those moments that I realized there is no one else I would rather want to quietly (and respectfully) annihilate a roach than with my younger brother. It's moments like this that are etched into my memory and will be retold to my kids when they plea for me to kill a bug. In the few instances where we weren't fighting for the TV remote but instead, corroborating over a mutual goal of terminating the roach lifeline, I'm glad we decided we were stronger united.

WHEN THAT WAS THEN, AND THIS IS NOW

During the 2020 pandemic, I was doing some deep house cleaning after I'd gotten bored of baking my third batch of banana bread. I ended up flipping through old photo albums that were tucked away on a bottom shelf of the bookcase. There were eight half-filled photo albums filled with photos tucked in laminated sheets.

The first page is filled with pictures of a bald baby boy in a baby rocker—I've been told, it is, in fact, me in these pictures. On the next page, the timeline skips ahead to seven-year-old me on my first bike, looking unamused and grumpy at the world. I'm convinced that as the years went on, my parents felt less of a need to document pictures of me and my fruit-roll-up-stained teeth. On the following page, someone scribbled May 4, 2000, with blue ink along the left margins. That was the day that my brother came into this world. Soon after, he became the new focus of the family pictures while I was in the background with my head pushed back from a nosebleed.

I spent some of my earliest memories in the living room of the house we still live in today. In one of these pictures, my three-year-old self is seen wrapping my chubby arms around my brother and resting my head on his tiny head. I am sporting an orange-striped top repping "Hello Kitty" while my brother is wearing an oversized striped navy polo. At the moment, I remember feeling so proud of my new title as "big sister" or in Cantonese, 家姐 (Ga Jie).

It's a strange yet comforting feeling to think back on the memories that once felt so free and full of innocence. The stain-ridden carpet was eventually ripped out and replaced with hardwood floors. The TV box, VCR, and DVD devices were replaced with a flatscreen TV and a Netflix subscription. My brother also finally grew into the polo shirt my mom had purchased for him fifteen years ago.

Nowadays, my five foot, two inches and three quarters self still feels the need to protect my five foot, eight inch karate-chopping younger brother. Regardless of how fast we both grow up, my first official job title on my resume is still "big sister." Although I was the older sister, there were many instances I looked up to my younger brother. I admire his athleticism, determination, endurance, and intelligence. As much as I tried to impart life lessons on him, I learned equally as much from him. Of course, I wouldn't admit this to him in person, but it is the truth. Even as adults, we still find an excuse to fight over the TV remote, but I wouldn't have it any other way. Because at the end of the day, we are still siblings after all, and there has to be some bites and scars to prove it. And if worse comes to worst, my mom still knows where she keeps her hangers.

TIME CAPSULE V

Read This for a Moment of Reflection

CHAPTER 12

Cup Half Full

Dear Grandpa,

I can't help but wonder what kind of life you would have had here in the United States if you were dealt a different set of cards. Would you be a world-renowned architect or would you be something—someone else? What if your language and culture weren't barriers but passageways for growth and opportunity? I wonder: What would be a greater risk? Choosing to move to the United States? Or choosing to stay in China?

I have so many of these hypothetical questions. I know I will never get a definite answer, but wherever you are right now, I hope you are safe, happy, and enjoying a cup of coffee with your morning newspaper. Maybe there is a translator up there in heaven who can read this story for you. If not, then I hope you can at least read this: 爷爷, 我很想你， 我也很爱你—Grandpa, I miss you and I love you. If I had one more chance to speak with you, I would remind you that you are loved and missed, even though you are not physically around. I would recount the memories and cherish them.

I will help you pour another glass of water and hold your hand one last time.

Love,
Your granddaughter Janette

WHEN IT WAS SUPPOSED TO BE THE BEST BIRTHDAY PARTY OF MY LIFE

There were ten of us locked up in a 200 square foot room.

It was supposed to be the night of "the best birthday party of my life." And it was, until my cousins and I were suddenly shoved into this 200 square foot room. The little ones were jumping over one another during a game of "The Floor Is Lava" and the older ones trying to prevent any traumatic head injuries.

I was very young at the time, maybe six or seven. My family hosted the birthday party at our house, and it was ten hours of lively chaotic energy. Some adults were chopping, dicing, and stir-frying vegetables in the heated wok, while others were huddled around the mahjong table. With each new round, the shuffling of the mahjong tiles created a comforting white noise ambience. The kids were jumping off the walls from the sugar rush fueled by an hourly dose of Fruit Gushers and a handful of Skittles. It was the type of exciting, infectious energy that would keep me up the night before.

Through the closed door, I could hear the sound of feet shuffling and stomping. The adults suddenly started raising their voices and even at six or seven years old, I could hear the panic in their voices. The entire time, I was standing at the foot of the closed door, trying to sneak a peek at the commotion through the door gap.

The older cousin in charge reassured me that everything was okay and nudged me to go play with the other kids. But I knew something was wrong. Everything was *not* okay; I knew when something felt off in my own home. I shrugged her off and sat at the edge of my bed listening intently to the raised voices on the other side of the door. The adults were speaking at each other in Cantonese, but the vocabulary they used felt foreign to me.

After the paramedics left and the shrieking turned into quiet whispers later, I found out that my grandpa had a stroke. I didn't know what that meant at the time or the severity of the situation, but what I knew was that grandpa was sick.

WHEN THINGS STARTED TO SHIFT

Like many kids living in transgenerational households, I was raised by my grandparents while my parents worked full time. In fact, up until I was shipped off to daycare at the age of four, Grandpa was the one who took good care of me. Although I was too young at the time to recall vivid memories with him, I wholeheartedly believed he looked after me, fed me, bathed me, clothed me, changed my diapers, and taught me how to hold a spoon in my hand. Since my grandparents were my primary caretakers, this was truly a testament to the adage that raising a kid takes an entire village.

In the photo albums showing my earlier years at home, I would be pictured sitting on my grandpa's lap with an ice cream popsicle in hand. He had a small bald patch at the center of his head and always wore a warm and pleasant smile on his face—a smile that greeted you like an old friend. His most prominent features were his short and thick bushy eyebrows, the same features passed down to my father, and now, to me. He was unbelievably kindhearted, introverted, compassionate, and loving to his grandchildren.

However, in the days after the incident, I could sense his overall demeanor and presence felt different. He was no longer that animated and upbeat grandpa I remember from the pictures. In more recent pictures, he would be seen staring blankly into the camera, emotionless and even slightly disconnected from the present. It was as if the stroke incident dimmed a fire inside of him.

During Chinese holidays, my family would gather to have dinner at a local Chinese restaurant. Around the round dinner table, the adults would catch up, laugh, and make comments about the giant king crab dish on the glass rotary table. On the other half of the table, my younger cousins, my brother and I would play our Nintendo DS or click, read, and scroll on our phones. Often, my grandpa would sit quietly at the table, listening but not contributing to the adults' conversation. He would let out a chuckle here and there, but he would mostly stay quiet and slowly eat the food my grandma put on his plate.

At these dinners, I would glance over and smile at him. Over the years, his remaining black hairs turned to gray and soon after, they fell off to reveal a nicely polished and reflective bald head. I would always wonder what was on his mind.

Was he happy that the family was all gathered around this dinner table? Was he also dissatisfied like the other adults about how the king crab dish were absurdly overcooked and salty? Or perhaps he didn't mind. Food is food, right?

Grandpa became a man of few words—someone who didn't feel the need to share his thoughts with the world but also wouldn't mind sharing if someone would simply care to ask.

WHEN "LATER" FELT GUARANTEED

Since the stroke impacted his physical mobility, Grandpa had to slowly learn how to walk again with a cane. It was much harder for him to walk long distances or even stand for a prolonged period of time. He became more and more sedentary with each passing day, and the weight accumulated from all meals packed with white rice and pork dishes.

Sometimes I could hear a soft thump and footsteps echoing throughout the house. I opened the door to the stairwell and saw him with one hand grappling onto the railing and the other on his trusty cane. He was trying to come upstairs to the second floor just to check up on me and see if I had eaten yet.

Even though we lived together under the same roof, he felt distant. My younger self only prioritized hanging out with friends or studying for the next test. To my younger self, my family was always going to be there when I get home, but that 75 percent spring sale at Aeropostale at the Kings Plaza Mall wasn't always going to be there.

"唔好挂住出去玩啦！应该留返喺屋企复习功课。"—"Don't go out and play so much; you should stay home and study more," he would repeatedly say to me.

"知啦，知啦，爷爷!"—"I know, I know, Grandpa." I would reply as I abandoned my schoolwork and dash out the door to hang out with my friends.

I would constantly try to justify my actions or *inactions*. *Grandma and Grandpa would always be there at home; I'll spend time with them later.* I would say to myself as I head out the door to go to the park with my friends. As the sun set, I would come back home, and they were in fact still there—sitting there in the same position that I last saw them in—sometimes with the day's Chinese newspaper in hand, other times Grandpa would be people-watching and simply staring outside the window.

My grandpa wasn't like the grandpa from the classic Disney movie *Monster House*. (Kenan, 2006) He wasn't the type to angrily scream at kids to get off his lawn and property. In fact, during the summertime, he would pull out a folding armchair, his little red footstool, and watch over the kids on the block. For hours, he would sit and watch as my brother, my neighbors, and I zipped up and down the block on our bikes.

"唔好行太远啊，衰人会拐走你噶。"—"Don't go around the block, or else there will be bad people who can kidnap you!" he shouted at us when we flew by him on the bikes.

"知啦!"—"We know!" I screamed back.

But as the rebellious kids that we were, we went around the entire block anyway up until the point where my grandpa could see us from where he was stationed in the front of our house. Then my neighbors and I would circle back around the block and come back the same direction we left from—as if we simply took our time biking up the street. When we returned, we acted normal, secretly trying to hide the heavy panting from the bike ride. As expected, Grandpa was still sitting in the same place we last saw him, with his eyes closed, back against the chair, and legs propped up on the red plastic foot stool.

WHEN LIVING ON BORROWED TIME

For twenty years, my world and my grandparents' world were separated by just a couple of wood panels. We all lived in a house that my grandparents and family had saved for since the day they set foot on this land. My grandparents' ceiling also acted as the floor and foundation for my parents and younger brother and me.

Even though we all lived in the same house, there was still an insurmountable language barrier between me and my grandparents. Since they didn't understand or spoke English, we communicated with each other through my conversational-level Cantonese. Our conversations never extended beyond the usual "I ate dinner already" and "School is fine."

When I was younger, I would blame our emotional distance on the language and cultural barriers. Yes, it was harder to communicate and discuss deeper topics given the language barrier. And yes, I inevitably gravitated toward the influence of American society and culture while neglecting the culture that was present in my own home. But nowadays, I cannot help but wonder where the line is drawn. Are language and cultural barriers justifiable excuses for my lack of initiative to strengthen an already frail relationship?

I may not be able to verbally communicate my feelings effectively, but I could at least *listen* and understand the general gist of their stories. It doesn't take much effort to just sit down and listen. More importantly, it was easier for me to enter their world than it is for them to enter mine.

I didn't realize the value of this missed opportunity until I left for college. On the weekends, I would come home and run downstairs to greet my grandparents. But even before I opened their door, I knew I could find them in their usual spots.

Since my grandma cooked the family's dinner meals, I knew she would be putting the finishing touches of garnish on the steamed fish in the kitchen, while my grandpa would be reading his daily newspaper from his chair by the living room window. I would charge through the door screaming,

"HELLO!" announcing my presence to the rest of the household. Grandpa, with his reading glasses on the bridge of his nose, would look up from his paper and greet me with a smile.

"你返来啦？"—"You've returned home."

I walked over to him and squeezed his hand.

"嗯"—"Yup," I said.

I nodded and plopped down on the couch next to my grandpa. He extended his left hand to me, and I held it with both of mine. His hands were rugged and covered in wrinkles with each line representing another year he escaped the inevitable. In the winter, his hands would feel toasty from being tucked into an electric heating pad. Other times, it would feel cold and cracked, which always warranted a concerned remark on my end. But even the chilly winter nights couldn't penetrate the warmth that radiated off my grandpa's hands.

Every week after I come home, he would ask:

"喺宿舍有冇食饱啊？"—"Do you eat enough at the dorms?"

"功课难唔难啊？小心身体，按时食饭训觉啊!"—"Is your homework difficult? Make sure to prioritize your sleep and health."

To which I would reply, "嗯，知啦"—"Mhm, I know."

Beyond these questions, he wouldn't inquire more into the specifics of my academics. He understood it was beyond my language abilities and something that I wouldn't want to discuss regardless. With my grandpa's left hand in the cusps of mine, we would sit in a comforting silence with our eyes faced forward at the TV screen with the silence broken by the sound of my grandpa's soft chuckle.

A few moments later, Grandma screamed, "食饭啦!"—"Dinner's ready!"—from the kitchen. I dashed to the kitchen to see what she had cooked up for dinner that night.

With a spare pair of chopsticks in hand, I began taste testing every dish while my grandpa would slowly make his way over to the kitchen area. As he walked down the hallway, I could hear the shuffles of his slippers as he grasped onto the hallway railing that he repurposed from an old mop handle.

A few moments later, he sat down in his usual spot and asked me to bring out the footstool from underneath his chair. He started sifting through the container of medications and handed me his ceramic mug.

"帮我斟半杯热水。"— "Help me fill up the glass half full with hot water."

Like all human beings, Grandpa was a creature of habit. Even if he didn't give me instructions, I knew to dutifully take the mug and walk over to the hot water boiler. I would carefully align the mug underneath the spout before I pressed the hot water button. Sometimes, I would overfill the mug past the halfway mark and pour some water back into the sink. Then I would set the cup on the counter and eyeball the water level again, to which I realized I poured out too much. Then I would repeat the process again until it is *perfect*.

After ten minutes of my little science experiment with the water boiler, I carefully walked back over and handed the mug over to my grandpa. He would then pour room-temperature water from the kettle into the same mug, resulting in a Goldilocks cup of lukewarm water. Like many Chinese people, Grandpa had a preference toward drinking warm or hot water because it helps with digestion, keeping the body temperature warm, and promoting blood circulation.

"What a genius," I would say to myself.

As I piled food on top of the bed of white rice, my grandpa would pop one pill after another from his various prescription bottles. I would occasionally pick out the best-looking meat from my grandma's dishes and put it onto his plate. In between gulps, he would nod to signify a thank you.

Afterward, I would trot back upstairs with my plate of food and sit myself down in front of the TV just in time for the 8 p.m. television shows.

Eating dinner with my family around a table was never a tradition in my house. My parents would arrive home around 9 p.m. to eat the cold dishes and pack the remaining for lunch the next day. As the years went on, my brother and I grew older and started eating dinner outside with our friends. That's when my grandma stopped cooking for us entirely because no one except my grandpa was ever home.

At the time, I didn't think much about sitting down at my grandparents' kitchen table and eating with them. To my younger self, my TV shows and friends felt more urgent and more important than the bonding time between myself and my grandparents. Today, nothing feels more urgent and important than our borrowed time together.

WHEN IT'S A REGULAR THURSDAY AFTERNOON

One day in mid-December 2018, I was sitting in my boyfriend Rauful's car, en route to Brooklyn from Manhattan. That day, Rauful was kind enough to drive me to Brooklyn for a work meeting. We were merely a block from the destination when my phone buzzed from the incoming text message.

I unsuspectingly tapped it open, thinking my dad sent another WeChat article about car seatbelt safety.

"Grandpa's in the hospital. Looks like he's not going to make it this time."

My heart dropped.

"Pull over," I said to Rauful.

I showed him my phone, and my eyes slowly welled up with tears until it filled to the brim.

My heart began pumping. First, at the pace of the car's blinking hazard lights but soon, faster and faster. My chest felt tight, as if someone had been slowly suffocating me from the inside out. All the while, I didn't even realize that I've been holding my breath. When I finally exhaled, the tears streamed down my face, blurring my vision, and flooding everything in its path.

My mind flashed back to all the "should have" moments. I should have eaten dinner with him more often. I should have held his hand a little longer. I should have just called home more. *Why didn't I just call more often?*

My mind began racing and filtering through every memory to try to recall the last time I said those three simple but powerful words to him.

[CTRL F]: "I love you."

N/A

[CTRL F]: "我爱你"

N/A

[CTRL F]: "Have you eaten yet?"

N/A

Everything around me felt disoriented as the walls of the car closed in on me—as if my whole world had shattered into a million fragmented pieces and I was tasked to put it all back together.

I looked back down at my paralyzed hands and forced myself to say something, say anything.

"Is he okay? What happened?" I texted.

Buzz.

"Grandpa had a heart attack. Come home soon, and we can go see him," he texted back.

In the car, the silence was deafening against the sound of the blinking hazard lights. With each passing minute, the ringing in my ears amplified as I buried my face into my hands.

"Let me take you home," Rauful said.

Going home was the only thing I wanted to do, but it was also the last thing I wanted to do. Going home meant everything was *real*. Going home meant this wasn't just some scary nightmare I have yet to wake up from. Going home meant I couldn't go downstairs to find my grandpa in his usual spot.

"No...I'm going to this meeting...since we already drove... all this way here," I muttered in between gasping breaths.

I knew my team was counting on me and I didn't want to let them down. With my damp sleeves, I quickly wiped off the remaining tears, then rolled them up to hide the evidence. Then, I flipped down the sun visor above me and stared at the girl in the mirror. She looked just like me. She looked at me with wet puffy eyes and a forced smile that could fool anyone, even me.

"It's just a regular Thursday afternoon," I said to her.

WHEN WE MAY MEET AGAIN

That evening, my father and I drove to the hospital in silence. The rest of my family had already seen him that afternoon, so I was the only one left to say goodbye. What felt like hours was actually only a twenty-minute ride but since my mind was racing at one hundred miles per hour, the car ride only made things feel more unreal and disoriented than it already was.

As we walked into the hospital, the air felt damp and stuffy, the kind of stuffiness I could feel in the back of my throat. The inherent maze built within a hospital didn't faze me. I've seen patients in hospital gowns and patients hooked on tubes and devices before, but nothing would have prepared me for seeing someone I knew, someone I loved, someone so close and personal lie still on the ICU bed.

I took a deep breath and walked into the lightly dimmed room. There he was, lying still surrounded by tubes and beeping machines. That past weekend, I dashed downstairs to relay a message that my dad had for my grandma. At the time, my grandpa had another complication on his foot due to his diabetic condition. His feet would occasionally swell, making it even harder for him to move around. He was getting up from the couch and I remember catching a glance from him before I headed upstairs. I remember thinking to myself, *I should go help him up and hold his hand.*

But I saw he had already gotten himself up. I was also in a rush to head out, so I quickly said hi and bye to both and went on with my day. Little did I know that glance would be the last time I ever got to see him again.

Back in that hospital room, I stood aside as my dad held onto my grandpa's hand and lightly kissed him on the forehead. My lips trembled and I could feel the wet, hot tears fill up my eyes as my dad tried to hold back his.

My dad gave a final squeeze to my grandpa's hand, turned around and said to me, "Say a couple of words to your grandfather."

He left me alone while he inquired about my grandpa's condition with the nurse on call.

My hands were already trembling when I took his cold hands into mine for the last time.

"对唔住，爷爷， 对唔住，对唔住，对唔住"—"I'm sorry, Grandpa. I'm sorry, I'm sorry, I'm sorry," I said while wiping away tears with my other hand.

"再见啦爷爷，我会永远爱你噶!"—"Goodbye Grandpa. I will always love you," I said again, hoping that somehow a miracle would happen, and he would reply and squeeze my hand back.

I didn't know if he could hear me, but I said a couple of words in English even though he wouldn't have been able to understand. I kept repeating those two phrases without letting go of his hand just in case he could actually hear me. His hand felt cold and clammy. The usual warmth he radiated slowly dimmed. But I held on anyway until it was time for both of us to go.

The next day, in the early hours of a Saturday morning, my dad received the phone call that confirmed my grandfather's passing.

I thought to myself that my grandpa had waited for me to visit him one last time before he went toward the light. I thought back to a line from the TV show *100.* This line is said whenever a loved one is leaving us to go to a better place:

"In peace, may you leave the shore, in love may you find the next. Safe passage on your travels until our final journey on the ground. May we meet again."

CHAPTER 13

A Phoenix Rising from the Ashes

Dear former self,

This experience came into the home inside you and shattered things you didn't know could be broken. As you were growing up, you were taught SOHCAHTOA and how to dissect an earthworm, but you were never taught how to safely process emotions and guilt. Instead, you learned that crying is a weakness and showing emotions is your Achilles heel. You never learned that your greatest strength is allowing yourself to feel. Before school started every September, you were told to get annual physical checkups. But you were never told mental health checkups are equally as vital.

Remember when you told Grandma that you had a sore throat? She made you a warm cup of honey lemon tea. Congested nose? She wrapped some cooked rice with ginger, microwaved it for twenty seconds, then rubbed it all over your face's T zone, neck, and behind the ears. Headache? You popped an Advil or two. For as long as you could remember, you were handed an eastern and western solution to every physical problem. And for every physical problem, you learned how to medicate.

But what happens when you are confronted with something as earth shattering as the death of a loved one? You yearned for a quick fix that doesn't exist. You were left with a broken home with no tools to rebuild. Instead, the solution is to feel the pain, to process the emotions, to surrender yourself to the crumbling world around you. Finally, on your own timeline, you gradually learned to rebuild a reality with a newfound self-awareness and gratitude, like a phoenix rising from the ashes.

From this experience, you learned the true definition of resilience and strength. You learned to not take things for granted. You were reminded everything is temporary. You learned that you have many homes, but the one you spend the most time in is within yourself—so you must look after it and cherish it. You don't need to build a fortress around a home that is stronger without barriers.

With love from your current, better self.
Janette

WHEN WHAT REMAINS IS STILL ALIVE

In the days following my grandpa's passing, everything felt disoriented. I couldn't tell if the world was spinning faster, or I had just become numb to the usual fast pace. But I forced myself to put one foot in front of the other and stumble my way back to my "normal." In the meantime, while my family was handling the logistics for the funeral, I was thrown headfirst into the midst of finals week.

I remember actively making the decision to keep this family matter to myself, unwilling to force my hand and play the "pity" card. Besides Rauful, no one, not even my close friends, knew about my grandfather's passing. Even as I write this story three years later, this untended wound hasn't been treated. My refusal to accept his death caused the heartbreak that has still not healed.

It was two weeks before Christmas, a holiday that I don't celebrate but I remember how eerie the city decorations seemed at the time. I was sitting in my dorm room by myself and was left alone with my thoughts, memories, and inescapable guilt. I was drowning in assignments and project deadlines along with the influx of finals that I have not begun preparing for. I remember staring at my laptop screen infuriated at my inability to focus on the task at hand, naively thinking to myself, *God, how inconvenient is the timing of all of this.* As if there was ever going to be a *convenient* time to mourn a family member's passing.

I began breathing heavily then sensed an oncoming panic attack. That's when I did something that still sends shivers up my spine when I think of it today.

I said to myself, *Don't think about it. Just dissociate yourself. Stop feeling guilty. Stop feeling sad. It's not important right now. What's important are your finals and deadlines.*

It was as if I reached deep into the hard drive of my brain and flipped the switch from manual to automatic. From being human capable of feeling human emotions to an automated robot incapable of processing emotions.

The disturbing part for me was that it worked.

Looking back, it's extremely terrifying to know that I was capable of turning off the very feelings that humans are endowed with. At the time, I didn't realize the extent to which this act of dissociating and suppressing feelings was extremely unhealthy and toxic to not only myself but to those around me.

I remember feeling a wave of relief when I realized the days of the funeral aligned with my finals schedule—as if I was lucky I could squeeze in this last-minute event in my already jam-packed finals week schedule.

Now I recognize that at the time, I wrongfully believed I was being mentally strong—that I was an independent woman who could successfully handle her own emotional baggage. I didn't want to transfer the burden onto my friends and force them to carry the weight already heavily crushing my chest. But looking back, I was exactly the opposite of what I thought I was. I was afraid of confronting my emotional baggage while also neglecting the support system I had. I chose the easier route, which was to force a smile on my face and go about my day as if the birds were still chirping and everything was normal—but it wasn't. Yet, what remains is still the very present, very alive, traces of guilt and regret.

WHEN ALL THAT'S LEFT ARE ASHES AND MEMORIES

After my grandfather's passing, everything in the house was the same, yet it felt so different. My grandma immediately started packing up his belongings and putting them into heavy-duty black garbage bags. Some were thrown away while others were donated to a local thrift shop. The holidays arrived with less festivity than the years past.

Even though my grandpa was never the talkative one in group settings, I couldn't help but notice his lack of presence. One less chair to set up, one less chopstick to layout, one less rice bowl to wash. The family went on as usual and I was left questioning whether *I* was the only one overreacting.

The topic and concept of death is very superstitious and taboo in Chinese culture. For instance, the pronunciation of the number four in Chinese is 四 (si4) is very similar to the pronunciation of the word "death" in Chinese, 死 (si3). That is why many Chinese families will go to great lengths to avoid this number from living on the fourth floor of an apartment to avoiding having a house number with the number four in it.

It's even considered taboo to gift a clock to another Chinese person. This is because the phonetic sound of the word clock in Chinese is the same as another word for death, "zhong."

Since many Chinese people believe in prolonging and preserving life, they believe that living in the presence of the number "four" welcomes the arrival of death itself.

This line of logic, in turn, encourages the lack of discussion and communication around this critical topic. The lack of discussion is grounds for the missed opportunity that brings family and loved ones closer together after a tragedy. Discussion brings closure. It brings clarity. It brings order amid chaotic memories, thoughts, the "what ifs" and the "should haves." Due to this "culture" in Chinese households coupled with language barriers, I was never able to find emotional clarity with the help of my family.

Two years later, a close friend and I were on an hour-long train ride commute back home to Brooklyn from Manhattan. I had just finished Paul Kalanithi's 2016 book *When Breath Becomes Air* and highly recommended it to her. After I gave her the general gist of the book, she hesitated and responded by asking,

"Are you afraid of death or dying?"

This was two years after my grandpa had passed, and I had never told her about it. Truthfully, I didn't know the answer to that question without opening that can of worms, so I deflected the question:

"I am afraid of...not living up to my potential...and not being able to do all the things that I want to do."

At twenty-two-years-old, I felt invincible. Like I'm standing at the top of the world, armed, and ready to take on the next challenge that life throws at me. Like I can dance without the fear of someone watching. Like I can jump without the fear of falling. Like I can fall even when no one but me, will catch me.

Although I deflected the question, the short and immediate answer to that question is, "No. I'm not afraid." The art of dying is a natural phenomenon that truly gives meaning to the phrase, "Life is fragile, and tomorrow is never guaranteed." In truth, what is the value of life without the certainty of death?

But who knows what my response would be if I were actually confronted with death? If the train we were taking suddenly derailed, perhaps my response would have been different in that moment. It's one thing to welcome death with open arms, but it's another thing when we are given an expiration date.

Despite all this talk about death, I am optimistic. I believe that my generation, the ABCs and others like us, are more self-aware than our ancestors. We have grown up around all sorts of cultural taboos. But at the same time, we understand the ripple effects of intentional avoidance. Instead of shying away from traditionally taboo topics like death and mental health, we choose to bring these topics to light—to take control of its impact rather than allow it to control us. We understand the cultural fear of death but even more so, we are becoming more self-aware to learn how to better mitigate the circumstances around this inevitable reality.

After going through this family tragedy, I realized that what I am afraid of isn't death itself. Instead, it is the fear of leaving my family and loved ones crumbling inside without the support system of having one another. To use *death* as a rational excuse for rejecting anything spontaneous or adventurous. And most terrifyingly, use *death* as a reason to not live in the present.

From this day forward, I want to always have the courage to pursue what sets my soul on fire. Because one day, that fire will slowly dim and only ashes and memories will be left.

TIME CAPSULE VI

Read This to Teleport to the Other Side of the World

CHAPTER 14

Free Range Chickens

Dear Mom and Dad,

Remember when I went to Beijing in the summer of 2019? When I was there, I learned about the term "放养鸡"—"free-range chicken?" Yes, Mom, it's similar to the organic eggs you normally buy in bulk at Costco. But I also learned this term has another meaning to mainland Chinese people.

放养鸡
fàng yâng jī

1. According to the National Chicken Council (yes, that is actually a thing), free-range chickens have access to the outdoors for at least some part of the day, whether the chickens choose to go outside or not. (National Chicken Council, 2021) In practice, most chickens stay close to water and feed, which is usually located within the chicken house. Chicken labeled as "organic" must also be "free-range," but not all "free-range" chickens are also "organic."
2. According to my experience in China and conversations with Chinese natives, "free-range chicken" is a term used

to describe what many Chinese people believe to be, the parenting style of "typical" American parents. This means that the American parents would have a more laissez-faire approach to their children in terms of their education and social life—similar to how a free-range chicken would live its life roaming freely from one side of the barn to the other.

During my stay in Beijing, you both continuously reminded me to visit the Great Wall of China. Besides the pictures of the UNESCO landmarks that I sent over through WeChat, I also unexpectedly learned about the American and Chinese education system as well as my role in between these two seemingly black and white worlds. Here is the story of what wasn't included in the pictures I sent over...

With love from over the great (fire)wall,
Janette

WHEN THE BEST ADVICE IS THE MOST OBVIOUS ONE

I first encountered this term, 放养鸡—free-range chicken, during my summer abroad in Beijing 2019 with the Princeton in Beijing Program, also known as "PIB." (You have to pronounce each letter separately. "PIB" should not rhyme with "bib") The program is even more commonly known as the *Prison* in Beijing program. This Chinese-learning program is notoriously known for its intensive eight-weeks curriculum that could whip up a student's Chinese abilities faster than an amateur baker whipping up egg whites using a hand mixer cranked into overdrive.

In the days just before I left for PIB, I spent hours on days stuffing the turkey that is my luggage. On the last day, my dad stood idly at the doorway, amused at how his five foot and three-inch daughter could own so much stuff. I looked up toward him to acknowledge his presence then returned to stuffing. Even though luggage space is like expensive New York City real estate, I am a firm believer that one should not purchase things one already owns. Over the years, I've taken on my mom's tendencies to overpack and be wary of all things included at the hotel.

"But Mom, the hotel has towels," I said.

"佢哋啲毛巾好污糟噶!"—"Yes, but their towels are dirty," she replied as she tossed in the Ziploc bag full of pain and diarrhea-alleviating medications.

She said the word "dirty" with a scrunched-up face, the same face I make when I'd accidentally bit into a string of ginger that hid in my congee.

I looked down at her overflowing luggage with the two large body towels sandwiched between the covers. First, I used my left hand, then my forearm, then my whole body, to hold the suitcase down while my right hand wrestled with the stubborn zipper. *Useless.*

I flipped over the cover again and lo and behold, tucked underneath the towels lie three white plastic hangers. I whipped them out and waved them in the air.

"酒店啲衣架好污糟噶，啲人用过晒"—"The hotel hangers are dirty, and other people have used it!" My mom argued as she sealed off another Ziploc bag with full-size shampoo and conditioner bottles.

So, in June 2019, as I was packing for not a week—but a year away in China, I found myself in a similar but not so similar dilemma: Should I pack the Ziploc bag full of pain and diarrhea alleviating medications or pack my handy dandy travel iron (for the catastrophic emergency that the one blouse I packed will get wrinkly)?

I mentally weighed the options. Do I...

A. Want explosive diarrhea and look put together with a wrinkle-free blouse?
B. Want mild diarrhea and bring shame for my family because people would think that my mom hasn't taught me how to iron?
C. Want a mild (but controlled) diarrhea and don't pack the high-maintenance blouse?

Answer Choice: C

As my dad watched my futile attempts to stuff, sit, zip, and weigh my luggage in repeat, he continued to hover. He was leaning against the door frame, with one foot halfway into the room preparing to give a good old life lesson speech. I, as the backbone of this entire assembly line, was getting increasingly frustrated my dad wasn't helping.

Finally, with his left hand on his hip and right hand waving a finger in the air, he said,

"Remember, if you want to get better at speaking Chinese, the best way is to speak more and talk with more Chinese locals."

I thought back to how I was told not to speak with strangers when we were younger. It also reminded me of the threats my parents used to tell me and my brother whenever we misbehaved and refused to speak Chinese at home.

"我哋送你返大陆畀你学一年中文"—"We are going to send you back to China for a year to learn Chinese," my dad would tease. At the time, the threat felt imminent and personal. In fact, it repelled me further away from learning the language.

Yet despite my reluctance to take Chinese lessons, piano lessons, and prep classes, all I had hoped for was to make my parents proud. I hoped my accomplishments could be an extension to theirs and that they beamed with a sense of pride when their friends wondered how I was able to travel on a full scholarship. But this trip to China felt especially different and personal. While I was glad my parents' ~~threat~~ wish was fulfilled, I felt proud I was doing this, for not only them but also for me—to see this experience as an extension of myself.

I nodded my head and said, "I know, I know." I let out a sigh.

I looked up again toward him, waiting to hear the rest of his "When I was learning English at your age..." anecdote. But he was already gone. I was expecting a speech about language learning, education, or speaking up. But what remained was just the sounds of his slippers trailing off against the hardwood floors. I gave one last hard push, leaning my entire body weight against the luggage until I heard a satisfying click.

The next night, as I whispered goodbye to the city of flickering lights, I reminisced about my Chinese learning experience. By summer 2019, I was at the three years mark of formally learning Chinese. So, at that point, my Chinese ability wasn't awful. But it wasn't great either. I wholeheartedly believed that even if I achieved "superior" language status, there was always room for learning and improvement, especially when it came to learning a foreign language.

My dad's advice stuck with me as I looked out and saw the plane dip into the clouds of the night sky. I thought about the one sentence of wisdom that my dad just left me with. Sometimes, the best advice is the most obvious one. We just must be reminded of what we already know.

WHEN IT TAKES A LIFETIME

This was not vacation. This was a language learning boot camp repackaged with a fancy ribbon that says, "Study abroad."

PIB wasn't just a simple eight-week vacation getaway to the other side of the world. It was supposed to be a launching pad to prepare me for another ten months in Nanjing, China, a former capital located four to five hours bullet train ride south of Beijing.

On that first day, the founder and director of PIB said something that echoed my feelings about the past three years of my journey.

"学一门语言是一辈的事"—"Learning a language is a lifetime endeavor." He said to the auditorium room of 200 foreign students and one hundred tutors. I swear, it sounds more commencement speech-worthy when he said it in Chinese, but the message was still crystal clear.

Truth be told, it was supposed to be a sad realization. Why spend eight weeks of your life to willingly put yourself through this hell on earth of a program? Eight weeks could've been spent at an internship where you would hope that the ass-kissing could lead to a full-time offer. Why spend eight weeks doing something that would take a lifetime, anyway?

This time, my own thoughts hit me. If this language learning process is going to take a lifetime anyway, why *not* spend eight weeks pushing yourself past your physical and emotional limitations to see what was on the other side of fear and comfort? Why *not* spend eight weeks alongside other language-learning junkies who are equally, if not more, as passionate about growth as you are? Why *not* spend eight weeks learning to sit at the edge of your comfort zone to finally confront years of insecurities and self-doubt?

It's going to take a lifetime anyway, so I might as well go down trying with sleep deprivation.

My dad would be happy to know that this program didn't even give me a choice, even if I decided to be a mime artist for eight weeks. Following the inspirational speech on orientation day, the director of the program led an auditorium room of 200 foreign students to sign a language pledge, promising that for the next eight weeks, we will be speaking, living, breathing, and even dreaming in Mandarin-Chinese. Any violation of this rule could result in getting expelled.

How embarrassing would it be if I came home to my parents asking why I was home after two days in Beijing? To which I would hesitantly reply, "I didn't know how to say, 'The bathroom is flooded' in Chinese."

Even before the first day, I started off on the wrong foot. After embarrassing myself and flunking the interview to be in the fifth-year student cohort (the highest of the cohorts), I was demoted to Level 4.5, a cohort that consists of twenty heritage speakers like myself. Heritage speakers are people who have grown up speaking Mandarin, Cantonese, or another Chinese dialect at home. (This includes many ABCs.) Little did I know this "demotion" was a blessing in disguise.

My sole intention upon attending this program was to improve my Chinese speaking, listening, reading, and writing abilities. However, I realized there is more much more to what was advertised in the program brochures. It is gaining a nuanced understanding of not only the interrelationship between American and Chinese culture but also the understanding of how my fellow Chinese-American classmates and I are indirect diplomats acting as the bridge between these two countries. Through insightful discussions with my classmates, my normal black and white perception of certain topics suddenly faded into an obscure gray. These issues are more complicated than what meets the eye. They are messy and interconnected but they have layers that are worth peeling back to be examined and understood from every perspective—just as a wise green ogre once said, "Onions have layers."

WHEN LIFE IS A MARATHON

It was halfway through the eight weeks program when the characters "放养孩子"—"free-range children" stretched across the PowerPoint slide. The topic of discussion for that day was the American versus Chinese education system. By that time, my fellow ABC classmates plowed through dense topics like freedom of speech (which is ironic, I know) and the American dream versus the Chinese dream.

Although my classmates and I were Americans with Chinese ethnic backgrounds, our experiences within the American education system were vastly different. I was curious to learn how my classmates' experiences in Oregon or Texas differed from my experience in the NYC public education school system.

With the six of us, we bounced stories back and forth. Our teacher listened in horror as I tried my best to recount my experiences of going through school shooting or bomb threat drills in elementary and middle school.

It's one thing to experience the American education system firsthand, but it's another thing to put the entire system under a microscope and view it as an entity. We all agreed the flaws in the American public school system are deeply rooted in segregation, equity, and lack of funding issues, just to name a few. But once we become aware of what lies beneath the surface, it's impossible to unsee it.

On one hand, we learned that the American education system values the development of "free-range children." This means a resounding "fuck yes" to individuality, critical thinking skills, and the overall holistic development of children.

To American parents, it's important their children learn how to be independent and carve out their own path. But on the flip side, this "free-range children" mantra disseminates into a fragmented education system, lenient study habits, and the belief that their participation trophy will automatically land them a spot in a top job or college.

On the other hand, the Chinese education system is saying "fuck no" to all of the above. Instead, the Chinese education system highly emphasizes rote memorization and academic achievements. This is because education is flagged as a top priority within Chinese culture. In a country of 1.4 billion people, education has the potential to lift a family out of poverty within the span of one generation.

In class, we also learned that many Chinese people believe in the concept that one must not lose at the starting line—"不能输在起跑线" Especially when life is a marathon, Chinese parents will do everything in their power to ensure their child is one step, if not a mile, ahead of everyone else. In some cases, this would include the act of "走后门"—"Going through the back door"—where parents would bribe or money launder to get their children in an elite school.

If we were to compare these two systems in terms of snacks, it would be along the lines of this: The Chinese education system is the generation of uniform crackers that are nicely packaged in a factory assembly line, while the American education system encourages children that they can be whatever they want. If they despise the taste of dry cardboard, they can be a cupcake or a nutrition bar, one that is sugar-free, non-GMO, vegan, organic, naturally packed with twenty-seven minerals found at the local hipster café. The limit does not exist.

Of course, this all sounds like a huge generalization to pour salt on the divide between American and Chinese systems. To my American friends, the Chinese system strategy toward education may even seem ineffective, restrictive, and extreme. To my Chinese friends, they would say the same for the American system. This is all based on my shared findings and conversations with native Chinese people and American students as a self-appointed indirect diplomat. But at the end of the day, all parents, regardless of backgrounds, would agree their child is their top priority. So, parents would do what they can (based on what they know) so their child could receive the best education.

WHEN PRACTICALITY IS A METRIC FOR SUCCESS

I like to think that growing up as Chinese-American has allowed me to have the best of both worlds. Selfishly, I reaped the benefits of the American and Chinese education system. By day, I was running around the barn as a young and wild, free-range chicken, absorbing all the white lies about how America was "founded" when Christopher Columbus sailed the ocean blue in 1492. By night, my parents planned a 9 p.m. to 1 a.m. math lesson on their own. This resulted in a sobbing session because young optimistic Janette just couldn't grasp the concept of negative numbers.

Yet in between the Saturday school, summer school, and sobbing sessions, my parents instilled in me the value of education and learning. Like many Chinese immigrant parents, my parents are practical people. Education, whether it is through a public school system or additional prep classes, is a no brainer. In their view, education is the "easiest," most guaranteed, and foolproof route to success. The Chinese god of education would probably agree that the more degrees one collects, the more zeros one would have in their paycheck—practical.

When my parents immigrated to the United States for the abundance of opportunity, they too, wanted me to reap the practical benefits of the American education system. Yet paradoxically, they would get mad at me for developing those critical-thinking skills to question our society at large.

"Caring about the environment is not your job, it's the government's. Carrying around an inconvenient metal straw and needing to wash it at home? Not practical." They'd continue to say.

For the longest time, I too believe in their perceived value and practicality of education. Even me writing this sentence and my ability to string together semi-coherent thoughts is a beneficial byproduct of education. Admittedly, it's a tough act to balance. On one hand, I juggle with the American influence, and its individuality, critical thinking skills, and its "freedom first" mantra. On the other hand, there's the Chinese influence and its collective beehive mentality, hardworking nature, and "education first" mantra.

It's important to address a core shortcoming in both systems: the limitations of the traditional definition of education and its apparent fast pass to success.

Today, my nature to question the status quo forces me to recognize that "success" is subjective and there are many paths to success besides the traditional route. In truth, I believe that education truly begins after we graduate. This thought became more apparent after I navigated through seventeen years of schooling. Like many twenty-two-year-old recent graduates, we collectively sell our souls via job applications then say, "So now, what?" Now, is the time to venture outside the cage that was built to keep us safe. But in reality, the safest route is for us to learn continuously, roam endlessly, fail gracefully, just to get up and try again.

Whether it is learning a language or learning how to climb the corporate ladder, learning, in and of itself, is a lifetime endeavor. So why *did* I spend eight weeks doing something that would take a lifetime, anyway? Because eight weeks will fly by regardless, and time doesn't wait for anyone. Time is invaluable so it's up to us to decide how we want to spend it, based on our own metric of success.

As I continue to balance the values of the American and Chinese education system, I am grateful for my parents, who raised me to value the art of education and tolerated my progressive thinking (even if this conflicts with their traditional Chinese values). Even more so, I feel fortunate I can roam freely as an educated bilingual chicken in the in-between.

CHAPTER 15

When in Rome

Dear Mom and Dad,

Do you remember when our family vacation plans were canceled in August 2014? Dad, I vividly remember you suddenly whipped out the iPad, opened Google Maps, and traced the I-95 highway that ran along the east coast. It only took you ten seconds to say to Mom, "Get the luggage; we are leaving for Florida at 9 a.m. tomorrow instead."

I still can't believe we drove the fourteen hours straight from NYC to Orlando, Florida. Of course, by "we" I mean you both. Even though I was sixteen and Derek was fourteen, we both still complained in the backseat asking, "Are we there yet?" every twenty minutes.

I didn't know how to express it at the time, but that decision went against all the fibers of my core being. Mom, you had instilled a sense of over-planning and over-preparing for as long as I could remember. How were you so calm when we didn't even know where we were going to sleep that next night? It made me wonder where the line is drawn between spontaneity and impulsiveness.

Little did I know, this trip changed my entire perception of traveling for the better. You taught me how to pivot and be open to change and new possibilities. I kept this in mind when I had to navigate all the uncertainties of traveling abroad alone. I also recognized that our ability to travel comes from a place of privilege, in the form of time, money, and school scholarships.

Whether it is a last-minute road trip to Disneyworld or a ten-day pre-planned Chinese tour bus trip to mainland China, I would look forward to our vacation week every year. But after our family trips and my travel abroad experiences, I realized that traveling is more than posting pictures to impress middle school classmates on WeChat or Instagram.

Traveling is entering into someone else's world, their realities. It's being open and receptive to their culture, food, religion, thought process without colonizing their beliefs. It is an exchange of culture, arts, language, communication, and understanding. When we travel, we inevitably leave a piece of ourselves in the country and borrow a piece to take back with us to share with others.

When's the next road trip? I'll start packing.

Your chauffeur,
Janette

WHEN MASTERING THE ART OF THE SQUAT

In Chinese, there is a famous cheng yu called 入乡随俗. Cheng yus are the four-character proverbs or the idioms of the English language. It's the equivalent of the English proverb "When in Rome, do as the Romans do," or in my case, "When in Nanjing, do as the Nanjingers do."

In September 2019, this was the mantra I lived by during the first month of assimilating into my new life in Nanjing,

China. By following this mantra, I had to do as the locals do by conforming to the local Chinese customs.

So, if the local Chinese people use WeChat to pay for all purchase transactions, then I'd happily scan QR codes at the convenience of this cashless society. If others drink only hot water even in ninety-five-degree days, I will get myself a glass and set it down next to the air conditioning unit for three hours. Lastly, if everyone else uses the squatty potty, then I will gladly gather up my skirt like a tutu and get into a helicopter squat position.

While I was in Beijing that summer in 2019, it took me three weeks to master the art of the squat. Most of the public toilets in mainland China are holes in the floor. The only exceptions are in shopping malls and fancy hotels. As for the rest, I had to squat to do number one, number two, and number three.

Since China bathrooms do not provide toilet paper, it also took me a while to remember to carry around packets of tissue for toilet paper. In those three weeks, I gained a new sense of patience and balance. I learned to hover low enough so I don't splash the girl in the stall next to me, but high enough so an innocent bystander doesn't have to pull me out of the hole in the ground.

By the time I arrived in Nanjing in the fall of 2019, I thought I had gotten this squatting shit in the bag—that is until my phone slipped out of the kangaroo pouch I made with my shirt and I had to fish her out of the toilet hole in the floor.

Luckily, I hadn't done number one, two or three yet so it was just me versus my phone dipped in toilet water. I stacked so many layers of tissue napkins on top of one another that it started to look like the foundation of a Lady M green tea crepe cake. With a steady hand and skillful execution, I rescued her out of the hole and scrubbed her down in the sink for fifteen minutes.

入乡随俗, I sighed.

WHEN LIVING WITH THE LOCALS

Living in China, and traveling in general, always sent my entire being into a sensory overload.

Ooooh let's go see that. Let's eat that. Let's go down this dark alleyway and see where it leads.

As diversified as NYC is, this fascination was a byproduct of the fact that I grew up sheltered in the NYC bubble. I knew how to get from point A to point B with the help of Google Maps and English as my native tongue. I relied on my English like a crutch, and I knew how to play the game to live by the bougie high living standards of New York City.

But once I landed in Nanjing, China, the game board was yanked out from underneath me and replaced with another. I had so many questions, but the instruction manual was now backward, written in Chinese and no, I checked, there were no pictures.

Less than twelve hours after touching down in Nanjing, I arrived at the Nanjing University campus with a fat wad of official documents in hand. Already, the office was chaotic but luckily, the program coordinator at the school made acclimating to this foreign country a lot easier.

She handed me a paper with a checklist of things to do. First thing on the agenda: apartment hunting.

"你现在要做的是到楼下找你的地产经纪张师傅，他在等你"—"Here's everything you need to do. Go downstairs, Mr. Zhang, your realtor is waiting for you," she said, nudging me out the door.

I nodded and held the white sheet of paper in front of me, mentally translating words based on context clues.

Downstairs, I found a man in his late thirties or early forties standing idly by his electric moped.

"您好，您是张师傅吗？"—"Hi, are you Mr. Zhang?"

"嗯，你坐在后面吧"—"Yup, climb onto the back."

I looked down at his moped then looked back up at him.

"这里？现在?"—"Here? Now?"

"嗯"—"Yup." He was already in his seat and started the ignition.

I looked down at the eight-by-twelve seat and looked down at the dress I was wearing.

入乡随俗 —*Do as the Romans do*—I said to myself as I climbed on and tucked my dress underneath me like a diaper. *God bless my paranoia for reminding me to wear shorts underneath dresses.*

And just like that, we zipped away over cobblestoned roads and potholes, with my one hand gripping fiercely on the side handlebar and the other hand clenching the back of this stranger's denim jacket. All the while I was trying to be careful that my dangling legs wouldn't get struck by the incoming traffic. It felt like we were driving in the reverse direction of the Mario Kart track at 150 CC and Koopa, the cloud guy, is holding up a U-turn sign, telling us to turn around.

Amid all this commotion, my realtor started making small talk.

"你要找什么样的房子?"—"What kind of apartment are you looking for?" he asked.

"两方一厅的"—"Two bedrooms, one living room."

I replied, "So that I could also live with my Chinese tutor."

"嗯你的预算呢?"—"I see. What's your budget?" he asked while swerving around a man struggling to bike uphill.

I was armed and ready for this question.

"2,500 RMB" (ren min bi, the official currency of the People's Republic of China), I replied with a confident yet assertive tone.

I had prepared to give out a conservative number in fear of getting "jipped" because I was a foreigner. I heard so many horror stories about prior foreign students getting scammed because they weren't aware of the local customs or offered too high of a budget estimate.

"Hmm, 2,500的两房一厅有点难找"—"Hmm, that's going to be hard," he replied. "There are also very few apartments left since you arrived so late."

I knew he was playing the urgency card to get me to commit faster, but I wasn't folding. I stayed silent, unaware that my mouth was wide open, partially in awe of the shifting scenery, partially oblivious that I was catching all sorts of flies.

"你是中国人吗?"—"Are you Chinese?" he continued to ask.

"我是华裔。我家是广东人，但我是在美国出生长大的 。"—"I'm Chinese-American. My family is from Guangdong, but I was raised in America."

"哦明白了"—"Ah, I see," he said.

"你知道 。。。" —"You know...." he continued. "许多留学生来到中国的时候不太习惯" —"A lot of foreign students come here, and they aren't accustomed."

"习惯什么"—"Accustomed to what?" I said, suddenly realizing my mouth was dry from being opened so long.

"就是他们不太习惯我们的生活方式，不同的标准，你明白我的意思?"—"Different...way of living. Different standards, you know?" He unexpectedly made a sharp right turn. I almost flew off the bike and became roadkill.

"嗯"—"Mhm," I replied with a closed mouth.

"我们到了"—"We're here," he said, turning off the ignition.

We arrived at the back entrance of several seven story apartment buildings. The paint on the buildings faded into shades of muted pink and yellow; windows on every floor were surrounded by a cage of stainless-steel bars. To my right, a dozen other mopeds were parked underneath an outdoor canopy made up of scrap metal. To my left, several U-bikes were stationed along the wall. One of them was missing a seat.

I hopped off the bike and put on my best "I am not distraught at all" face. He pointed toward an open staircase.

"没有电梯"—"No elevators," he said.

He led me up not one, not two, but *six* flights of stairs. I had one of those *That's So Raven* moments where I foreshadowed myself lugging two fifty-five pounds of overweight luggage up the stairs. I was warned by friends that this type of cardio workout would happen in ninety-degree heat. But like committing to the 5 a.m. wake-up club, things always sounded easier in theory.

When we finally arrived on the sixth floor, I was huffing and puffing. Another older lady in her sixties was already waiting at the door and I greeted her in between breaths.

"这里是厨房 。。主卧。。第二个房间 。。"—"Here is the kitchen...the master bedroom...the second room...," she said.

I caught those keywords in between her heavy dialect accent. I couldn't understand half of what she said, but I smiled and nodded anyway. I looked up and noticed the water damage on the ceiling but didn't say anything.

In China, it's normal for two-bedroom apartments to have one master bedroom for the parents and a smaller bedroom for the child. In this first apartment, the second bedroom was just large enough to swing the door halfway open until it slams against the twin-sized bed. It made me uncomfortable that my tutor would have to live in this closet while I had the luxury of a master bedroom.

But the master bedroom was the size of my living room and kitchen in Brooklyn, *combined.* It even had an indoor patio, the place where many Chinese people could air dry their laundry.

I sat down on the mattress and just as expected, it was harder and more uncomfortable than the cardboard seats on Spirit Airlines.

From the window of the master bedroom, I could see the other apartment buildings. The buildings were worn down and shabby, but they still stood tall. I glanced down at a local who parked his moped under an awning. From the corner of my eye, I thought I saw a rogue chicken.

"这里还可以，我们看别的吧 。"—"This one is okay, but let's go see some more," I said to my realtor.

My realtor nodded, and we walked down the six flights, climbed back onto his moped, and once again, bolted away into the traffic.

With each new apartment he showed me, I grew more and more certain I had to let go of my NYC comforts and standards.

After walking up another six flights, I walked into a similar looking apartment. It was a decent looking place at a decent location close to campus, but two things felt off.

The layout of the place was like an escape room. In order to go into the master bedroom, I would have to go through the smaller "kid's" bedroom.

The location of the fridge was not where it's supposed to be.

It is awkward enough that I have to get permission from my Chinese roommate every time I go in and out my room, but this second point was a fuck no from me.

At the apartment, I stared at my realtor, stared at the oversized stainless-steel fridge, and stared back at him.

I waited for him to say something, but he just stared at me.

Silence.

"为什么这个冰箱要放在主卧里呢?"—"Why is there a fridge in the master bedroom?" I exclaimed.

I began to think this was all some huge simulation controlled by a seven-year-old playing the Sims video game on planet Mars. She figured out how to decorate her bedroom to include a fridge as the centerpiece, and I just discovered her latest creation.

"厨房没地方, 所以就要放在这里"—"There's no room in the kitchen. So, we put it here!" he immediately replied. He said it as if it was common sense.

"还有别的吗?"—"Any other apartments?" I asked.

This last apartment was in a fifty-something floor high rise located farther from campus. It was everything that my New York City heart desired. Modern furniture, floor to ceiling windows, views that overlooked the city—it was the whole package wrapped in bows and ribbons. Sure, I would have to set aside fifteen minutes to wait for the elevator and the rent was a bit higher but to me, this was the equivalent of living in a penthouse on Park Ave.

Despite all the enticing features, something felt off. Even though the high-rise apartment was everything I wanted, it felt disconnected from the rest of the city. It felt disconnected from my purpose of coming to this foreign country. I knew that if I wanted to live like the locals, I had to sacrifice a bit of my discomfort and inconvenience. With my budget, I couldn't change the reality of these apartments I could afford, but what I could change was my perception of it.

A six-floor walk-up without an elevator? → "It's good exercise. Consider it also as strength training when you have to drag a drunk friend up the same six flights of stairs."

Not accustomed to China's preference for extra-firm mattresses. → "They're better for your back anyway. The more uncomfortable it is, the more likely you won't sleep in."

Chipped paint from water damage? → "Remember that interior design inspiration you saw on Pinterest? It's the same difference. Say hello to the new textured wallpaper aesthetic of the year."

So that night, after making a pro and cons list, I called my realtor and told him to put me down for the first apartment.

After signing the papers and paying six months of rent in cash up front, it took me three days to remember how to get back home to my apartment.

Google Maps was useless because one, it is banned and two, the address couldn't be found on Baidu Maps, the Chinese version of Google Maps. And so, I had to rely on my two gigabytes of memory to go up a small hill, walk down a side street, turn right into an alleyway, then wait until I came across rogue chickens to know if I'd arrived at my destination.

So much of this first month boiled down to figuring things out as I go and accepting the different realities of my mother's motherland. Sure, I was thrown into the world of adulting with a how-to manual written in Chinese. But this is what comes with the beauty of traveling and getting into the rhythm of living like the locals.

WHEN LIVING A DOUBLE LIFE

When I was living in mainland China, I felt like I was living a double life.

It's a strange realization to make, especially when I try to zoom out and imagine what I looked like 50,000 feet away among at sea of native Chinese citizens. At 50,000 feet, I looked like one of them. It's like playing a game of "I Spy" and the clue is to spot the ABC. It is nearly impossible—until I zoom in closer. (For my international friends, I would like to apologize on behalf of the rest of America and its outdated and inconvenient imperial system.)

At 500 feet, it's my New Yorker too-fast walking pace.

At fifty feet, it's the blonde balayage hair and the tanned skin from my reluctance to wear sunscreen.

At five feet, it's the nose ring I secretly got in Taiwan.

At five inches, it's the freckles from yet again, my reluctance to wear sunscreen.

If any of those things weren't obvious enough, the six-foot, one-inch Bengali boyfriend beside me was always a dead giveaway that I'm a 老外—foreigner.

But when I would go on my solo dates or pick up breakfast at the local 包子 (bun) stand, I think I looked just like any other Chinese native. While I didn't receive the same education or cultural experiences as native Chinese citizens, I found comfort in being surrounded by people who looked like me. I found solace in knowing that no one is ever going to inflict microaggressions like calling me "a chink" or telling me to go back to America. I was living a double life and I could thank my girl Miley Cyrus for the inspiration.

On one hand, I found comfort in knowing that I can easily "blend in" without drawing attention to myself. The blending in part got easier after I transitioned the blonde to brunette and I swapped the nose ring to a nose stud. But I couldn't help but feel like a spy. (Admittedly, this is an awful analogy given the supercharged and deteriorating tensions in United States-China relations.)

In this self-handled black operation, I had three things on the agenda.

- [x] Make small talk about the weather with Chinese locals.
- [x] Have deep talk conversations with Chinese locals (i.e., America's gun violence crisis).
- [x] Eavesdrop on conversations at coffee shops while pretending to listen to music.

Throughout these not-so-clandestine conversations, my Chinese ethnic roots allowed me to break past the "wall" usually between foreigners and Chinese locals. I traveled under an alias, and the locals spoke to me as if I were from their village assuming I was one of their own.

Yet, on the other hand, some days I wished I could "~~blend~~ stand out." So that I could make it socially acceptable to slap a big sticker on my forehead that says, "I'M A FOREIGNER. TAKE IT EASY ON ME AND MY CHINGLISH. PLEASE GIVE ME SPECIAL TREATMENT."

That way, this forehead sticker can serve as a disclaimer that I might not be 100 percent in tune with the conversation, not because I am being a rude bitch, but because I'm racking my brain to translate the phrases used in the conversation.

During the second week of Nanjing, I had the chance to "test the waters" by enrolling in elective courses at Nanjing

University. On the roster, an environmental sociology course caught my eye.

In Mainland China, the majority of the college courses are presented by one professor versus a lecture hall of 300 students. For the entire duration of the class, whether it is one hour or three, the professor is at the front of the room mumbling into a microphone. Behind him is his assistant, a lengthy eighty-three-slide PowerPoint with more text on the screen than white space.

The rest of the lecture hall is occupied with 297 Chinese students with their heads faced down in their textbook or phone. In the front row, my two other foreign classmates and I are digesting the firehose of information about epidemiology and global health.

When I walked into the room of my environmental sociology class, I expected nothing less than to fade into the background with 300 eager (but not that eager) college students. Instead, before I could even stop myself, I walked too confidently into a small room of five other students. On top of that, I was ten minutes late and had missed the first (and second) sessions of class. At that point, the five of them had already plowed through the ice breakers and declared their unassigned assigned seats for the rest of that semester.

Thirty minutes of me pretending to understand the material later, the professor called for a break. He was a tall, slim guy in his mid-forties. I immediately knew he was different than the other professors. Unlike the other professors, he didn't read from his PowerPoint, so he was my favorite. During the break, he made his way over to the back of the room.

"你是新来的学生吗?" —"Are you a new student?" he asked.

"是的，老师您好，我叫伍霖莉，我是从美国来的留学生。我想问一下我能不能旁听这门课?" —"Yes, my name is Janette Wu, and I am a study abroad student from America. I was wondering if I can audit your class as one of my electives."

I don't quite remember our conversation, but I remember tapping the table of the girl next to me afterwards.

"PST PST 你好，你有这门课的大纲吗?" —"Pst pst, do you have the syllabus for this class?"

"老师没有提供教学大纲"—"The professor didn't give us a syllabus for this class," she replied.

"哦，好的谢谢"—"Oh, I see. Thanks!"

"我也是个留学生"—"I'm also a study abroad student." *So she was eavesdropping...*

"真的吗"—"Oh REALLY?" I said. I lit up at the thought of being classmates with another ABC, naively assuming she was also from America.

"嗯我是从马来西亚来的。我在这里呆了一年多了"—"Yeah, I'm from Malaysia, but I've been studying here for over a year now."

"哇塞，马来西亚"—"Oh...wow, Malaysia!"

"我们有个微信团，老师会在那边跟我们联系。我可以把你加上去"—"The professor sends us updates through the WeChat class group chat. I can add you in."

She scanned the QR code for my WeChat username. With a click of the accept button, I beamed at the thought of making a new friend."

At the end of class, the professor announced that in the next class we were going on a fieldtrip. I was ecstatic. The third grader inside me lit up at the sound of my third favorite "F" word, behind "free" and "fried" (chicken).

A week later, the entire class (all six of us) met up to take the train to our field trip destination. I had assumed we were going to a museum, but to my disappointment, we visited a small lake on the outskirts of the city.

In the lake's defense, the scenery was beautiful. Placid waters, green mountains in the distance, and a handful of patient fishermen. And for a second, I forgot the lake was man made. As we walked around the entire lake, our only instructions were to "observe the scenery." An hour later, my professor huddled up the group to discuss our findings.

He pointed at the blown-up advertisement posters behind us. "Recently, construction began for a huge development project in the area to create a new school, malls, residential and commercial buildings." He said, "How do you think this will affect the landscape here?"

One of the male Chinese classmates from the group answered. My professor nodded and suddenly turned to the girl next to me.

"我们的马来西亚的朋友有什么想法呢?"—"What does our Malaysian friend think about this?" he said. In an instant, my palms started sweating.

She gave a B+ answer. and my professor nodded in acceptance.

At that stage, I was actively wiping my palms on the sides of my jeans when my professor turned to me and said,

"我们的美国朋友呢？你对这个话题有什么想法呢?"—"What about our American friend? What do you think about this?"

I laughed nervously as the rest of the class turned their attention on me. Maybe they were expecting some well thought-out, coherent, and elaborate explanation with an introduction, thesis, three supporting details, and a conclusion. Maybe they were just glad they were not being summoned to answer.

I wanted to share my thoughts on commercialization and the need to strike a balance between planet and profit. I wanted to regurgitate that Chinese lesson where we had a whole debate about economic development versus environmental protection. But all I managed to do was laugh nervously and let out a squeak. "我不知道"—"I don't know." I never wanted to throw myself in a man-made lake so quickly until that moment.

I laughed sheepishly again, hoping my professor can sense my hesitation to answer. This way we just move the fuck on and walk another lap around the lake.

Pick on someone else dammit, there are five other victims to choose from.

Silence.

I'm a foreigner. Please take it easy on me and give me special treatment.

But, to my disappointment, he just stared at me with his arms folded across his chest. The other students stared at me then back at him. And I stared at the ground, wishing I had inherited some superpower to melt into the cement below me.

What had felt like an eternity at the DMV later, he moved on.

And that was the last time I went to that class.

To this day, I remember this memory very vividly. They say that vivid memories are often attached to events with strong emotions. So, if I were to put a label on this particular event, it would be within my top twenty-seven painful and humiliating moments. Perhaps it was the thought that I was held at an astronomically higher standard because I was an ABC. That because I am an ABC, I am expected to perform better, to do better, to *be* better. If another one of my non-Asian classmates were with me in that class, would they be expected to answer? Or would they be praised for simply showing up to the class taught in one of the hardest languages to learn in the world?

After that spotlight experience, I wish I can say my desire to travel and chart the uncharted territories was stronger than my desire to play small. That my desire to carpe every fucking diem was stronger than my brain's self-defense mechanism to protect my fragile ego. That my desire to constantly strive toward personal growth is stronger than the hypothetical scenarios of "What if they judge the way I speak?" But the truth is, there are still times I am engulfed in the fears of judgment and criticism that I don't sound fluent enough compared to my fellow ABC or native Chinese peers. There are still times when all I want to be is hide in the shadows as an undercover spy with a black trench coat, a fedora, and a Manila folder with a red "classified" stamp.

WHEN I FELT LIMITLESS

When I was living in Nanjing, China in the fall of 2019, a conversation with my language tutor currently lives rent-free in my brain. Her name is Xue Fei, and she was a graduate student studying artificial intelligence. From the way she described it, it sounded super fancy, intimidating, and "Elon-Musky." But even after our first interaction, I knew how casual and down-to-earth she was. We immediately bonded because we shared the same last name too. Like all the other Chinese tutors that I've encountered, she was kind and receptive to learning more about American culture and my language learning journey.

It was one day during our early interactions in mid-October, we were chatting away in the student lounge. I noticed she was carrying an English test prep book.

“这是什么?”—“What’s that?” I asked pointing to the booklet that stuck out underneath her laptop.

“哦没什么”—“Oh, it’s nothing,” she said. She pulled the book out from the stack and handed it to me.

“我下个星期要考试，是英文水平测试”—“I’m studying for an English proficiency exam next week.”

“是吗? 如果你需要帮忙的话，我也可以帮你复习”—“Oh really? If you want, I can help you study for it too!” I flipped the booklet open to a random page and skimmed through the reading passage. I winced at the reminder of all the reading comprehension passages from SAT prep.

“你准备好了吗?”—“Do you feel ready for it?” I asked, closing the booklet.

She laughed and almost choked on the water she was drinking. “当然没有”—“Hell no!” she said.

“我上次练习英文的时候是在高中。除非他们是英文专业的或者想从事翻 译单位的，许多中国高中生毕业了以后没有机会接触英文。”—“I haven’t learned English since high school. Many Chinese students don’t engage with the language unless they are pursuing an English major or want to become a translator,” she continued.

“真的吗? 我们在美国的高中生也是一样的。我在高中的时候也“学过”几 年的拉丁文和西班牙语。”—“Wow, really?” I exclaimed. “I didn’t know that. It’s similar for us high school students in America. I ‘learned’ Latin and Spanish in high school.” I raised my hands to emphasize the bunny ears quotation marks.

“我的高中没有提供中文课，但如果有的话，我宁可上中文课。”—“My high school didn’t offer Chinese classes, but I would’ve taken it if I had the chance,” I continued to say.

“那你什么时候开始学中文呢?”—“Then when did you start learning Chinese?” she asked.

“我上大学的时候”—“In college...,” I replied. “我们每个星期要上 大班课，中班课，一对一课，连寒假和暑假的时候都要上课。”—“Through group classes three times a week, smaller group tutoring classes every week, and individual tutoring and every week for three years. During our winter and summer breaks too,” I explained.

Unbeknownst to the both of us, she opened a can of worms on this topic.

One thing led to another as I droned on about the constant insecurities of mastering a language I was already supposed to know. I opened up to her that despite the endless Chinese lessons, the fears of failures, judgment, and criticisms still simmered in the background. All of which was fueled by the constant comparisons between me and other Mandarin-fluent ABCs.

Throughout this hour-long conversation, she listened closely and nodded. And at the end of our session, she smiled and patted me on the back.

“别担心，你可以的”—“Don’t worry, you got this,” she said.

In the weeks following, our tutoring sessions always begin with “Do you need any help with this week’s lesson?” then almost immediately, we shift to an unrelated topic about filling in each other on the gaps between our respective cultures. Some days, I would spend thirty minutes explaining to her what “a meme” is, which would lead me down a rabbit hole of explaining every meme in my favorite memes Instagram folder.

“....Ohhhhh.” She clapped her hands together in acknowledgment. “我明白了”—“I get it now.”

I don’t think she got it.

But she was a good sport about it. My humor is on the spectrum of being self-deprecating, dark, and cheesy—so I get she might not have got it.

Other days, she showed me a Chinese song that's all about the "rings" in Beijing (NYC's equivalence of boroughs). The song was hilarious and catchy and sooner or later, we started singing the chorus to make each other laugh.

In between the memes and singing sessions, we dove into deeper topics like what it's like to move away from home and pondering questions like, "What does happiness mean to you?" These were the type of abstract, philosophical, brain-picking conversations that reminded me why I decided to dedicate four years of my college career to learning Chinese. These were the types of conversations that allow me to connect with others on a deeper level—to really understand how they think, their core values, and how they perceive the world. Learning Mandarin-Chinese became a gateway for me to step into their world when it wasn't easy for them to come into mine.

However, this journey of learning Mandarin-Chinese was never smooth sailing. From that first day of summer classes with the Flagship program in June 2016, it was an uphill battle and I've been barefoot, hungry, constipated, and carrying a thirty-pound bag of rice on my back the whole way.

By the fall of 2019, three and a half years since I started formally learning Mandarin, I was proud of my progress. Talking about both pop culture and worldly topics with my Chinese tutor, Xue Fei, is exactly how I envisioned my ideal foreign student self to be. During those tutoring sessions, Xue Fei listened attentively. She would occasionally nod her head while I attempt to explain my frustration through poorly drawn diagrams.

In her response to my rant about the American education system, she mentioned a 成语 (chengyu).

"那句成语怎么说来着?"—"What does that proverb mean again?" I asked.

She tilted her head to the side and looked confused at how I didn't understand *one* out of the 5,000 chengyus that exist in the Chinese language.

A few neural connections later, she immediately explained it: "啊，我的意思是。。。"—"Ah, that means..."

"你刚才怎么看起来有点困惑?"—"Wait, why were you so confused a few seconds ago?"

"我刚忘记你不是本地人，我们通常会用这个成语。"—"I forgot that you weren't a native Chinese because it's a really common Chinese proverb."

"啊？是吗?"—"Really?"

"对啊，……就是本地人。" —"Yeah, if I wouldn't have known you were a foreign student, I would've thought I was just speaking to a native Chinese friend."

"真的吗?"—"Really?"

"对啊"—"Yeah."

I beamed with joy. That one line. That one sentence of affirmation was all my body needed to release three years' worth of dopamine into my bloodstream. I know I shouldn't measure my progress off another person's beliefs, but man, the power that one line can do to boost my deflated ego. Forget all those negative doubts about "not sounding fluent enough." Forget the expensive piece of paper that says I majored in Chinese. I had gotten the official stamp of approval from a native Chinese speaker, and I felt fucking limitless.

That night, after I biked home on my U-bike and happily skipped up six flights of stairs with my phone flashlight in hand, I laid on the brick that is my mattress and stared up at the chipped paint on the ceiling. I was euphoric.

Traveling has allowed me to connect with others and myself in more ways than one. It made me question how I got used to taking the path of least resistance. But thanks to my parents, traveling has expanded my horizons, altered my perception of what I considered as reality, and sought to create more human-to-human connection, one conversation at a time.

Read This When You've Read Everything Else

EPILOGUE I

A Final Letter from the Author

Dear Readers,

I read somewhere that epilogues are the place to be brutally honest with the readers—to lay it all out on the table, tie up loose ends, slap a red bow on the cover then say TA-DA, I did it—now shower me with praise and affection. But before we cue the confetti, I have a few more confessions to make, so here it goes:

CONFESSION #1: I AM AN ADRENALINE JUNKIE.

There's something about dancing in that gray area of life and (potential) death that releases a shit ton of dopamine into my bloodstream. That's probably why I gravitate toward outdoor activities like biking (even when NYC taxi drivers play by their own rules), surfing (even when I saw shark fins in the distance), and skydiving (even with the possibility that the parachute might not open at 40,000 feet).

When I was in high school, my friends and I took a trip to Six Flags, an amusement park in New Jersey. The prime attraction was the King Da Ka, the tallest and fastest roller-coaster in North America. The ride lasted fifty seconds and all it did was shoot straight up forty-five stories from zero to 128 mph in 3.5 seconds. Then it drops you.

I waited in line for an hour and a half. And for the entire ninety minutes, I was shaking from the nerves like a wet chihuahua, blaming the burst fire hydrant underneath my armpits on the summer heat.

I hated the anticipation. I hated standing in line. I even hated how enthusiastic the sixteen-year-old operator sounded when he said, "Have a great ride!" as he pressed the red release button.

Ten seconds later, I am hit with a zero-gravity feeling that I can only describe as the feeling of being excised out of my body.

What I didn't hate, but instead, *reveled* in, was the after-glow. It's me patting down every limb on my body and screaming, "I did it! I'm alive!" It's me pointing at the behemoth of a rollercoaster afterward and saying, "I conquered *that*. And it only took fifty seconds of courage."

On a similar note, I thought that writing this book would only take fifty seconds of courage. Now that I'm on the other side, I've realized that "fifty seconds of courage" was the fattest lie I've ever told myself.

Instead, it only took me fifty seconds to talk myself out of writing every day for the past year. Majority of the time, I was shaking, screaming, and free falling into the pit of frustration and imposter syndrome, all the while doing my best to dodge the writer blocks. On some days, I would hypothesize the 1,000 reasons why I should press Ctrl+A and trash the entire book. Those days, I would eat my weight in cool ranch Doritos and cry in the shower to save tissues.

But on other (better) days, I would be galvanized by a burst of untapped realization—that I don't need to believe in myself to take action. In those moments, I'd recognize that *I* was the one who had control of the trigger release—not my sixteen-year-old insecure self. That at any moment, I can pull the trigger and dive full speed at all the feelings that used to paralyze me. To propel 128 miles per hour past the fragmented memories, doubts, and insecurities, only to come out on the other side to revel in the afterglow of writing another chapter.

"I did that. I'm alive. I conquered that with courage."

CONFESSION #2: I AM A RECOVERING PERFECTIONIST

After spending most of 2020 talking to myself and writing down my thoughts, I am left pondering about my next chapter. When I began this book journey in June 2020, I thought that writing this book would help me figure my past self out. I even joined therapy to help me clean out the leftovers that have been rotting in the fridge for many years.

The sessions only lasted a few months, but the process and habit of introspection stuck with me. And surprisingly, it worked.

The expired milk? Yup, that's chapter thirteen.

The bagel with cream cheese I swear is "still good." Chapter eight.

Then in August 2020, three months after I started my book journey, I'd written half of my manuscript. I told my developmental editor, Katie, how I felt like I barely scratched the surface for what I wanted to say. That even with an outline of a list of twenty potential topics, I am only shaving the tip of the iceberg.

As a female Asian American author publishing a book in a predominantly white dominated industry, it is inevitable that I feel a heavy burden and even urgency to cover all grounds and "be the voice" of my community. To highlight Chinese culture and heritage in a positive light, while shedding light on issues such as impostor syndrome, the immigrant trans-generational gap, coping with death, and other topics normally overlooked.

As I am writing this in May 2021, my initial statement still stands—I'm only at the tip of the iceberg.

But the only difference is that I've come to terms with the book feeling "incomplete." I'd realized that publishing a "complete" book is on par with chasing perfection—chasing that pot of gold at the end of the rainbow—but forgetting that the goal should be to enjoy the sight of the fucking rainbow.

After spilling over 50,000 words and an equal number of hours into this book, I feel like I am in a better place, a place where I feel fulfilled and blessed to have come this far. It's an extremely gratifying feeling to witness the process of transforming thoughts into stories, chapters, and now a published book. I learned how to piece together the scattered memories, relive the darkest moments, and lean into doubts, fears, and vulnerabilities—a process that I challenge you to try—but it is not for the faint of heart.

CONFESSION #3: I AM FLAWED AND THAT'S OKAY BECAUSE I AM HUMAN

As I am sitting here, writing the conclusion at the same place where I started my introduction, I am struck with what else I want to say. I figured I really screwed myself over by deciding to write a memoir at twenty-two. Because now I am confronted with the impossible task of figuring out how to write an ending to a story I am still living.

The thing with memoirs is that they only show a snapshot of a person's life. They are a glimpse of curated memories and a crystallization of certain viewpoints. They give you, my reader, a quick glance into the window of a flawed soul. In these final pages, here's everything I tried to—but can't edit out. Where do I even begin?

Do I mention the hesitancy I still have with language learning? Perhaps I should mention how no one has anything figured out but we assume that everyone around us has it all together? What about the transgenerational gap that still threatens the silent treatment while living in my childhood home? How about the years of unlearning certain habits and triggers?

As humans, we are naturally flawed. But this doesn't make us any less worthy of others' love and connection. We tend to connect more with others who are similar, whether that is in the forms of interests, experiences, beliefs, values, etc. We tend to consider those with similar stories in upbringings and struggles as extensions of ourselves.

I believe that the reality and beauty of any creative work lies in its open interpretation. I hope that, as you were reading this book, you were able to find some aspect of yourself in these stories—that in the spaces between these lines, you were able to feel seen and heard. That even if it was just for a moment, I was able to help carry some of your burden so you feel lighter and take another step forward.

This book is only the beginning of my lifelong legacy project. I challenge you to start yours—to share your stories even if no one is listening yet. To be courageous in your pursuit of what sets your soul on fire. To lean into your fears and insecurities. To lean into your vulnerabilities. Because when you do, those around you will do the same—and that will make all the difference.

From the author and your biggest fan,
Janette

EPILOGUE II

'Dear Janette' Written by Dad

2021年6月25日

我们的家族与你和弟弟的成长

亲爱的女儿, Janette,

按你要求, 今天讲讲我们的背景, 让你知道你是从哪里来的, 也让你更了解每一代不同的生活方式与文化的差异.

我和你妈都是来自中国南方的一小城县, 它的名字叫台山, 一个非常出名, 美丽的地方, 第一批来美国的中国人就是来自台山。关于家族成员, 我们只能从你爷爷那一代开始讲了,前几代的我了解不多。你爷爷有两个兄弟和两个姐姐.你爷爷是最小的一个。你爷爷出生在一个小镇, 叫冲蒌。其他几个兄弟姐姐都是在农村出生。

据说在1930年代时, 因为村与村之间有纠纷, 他们的村庄给火烧了, 所以整个村庄都搬出来小镇住。你爷爷是高中毕业的, 在那个年代很不容易了, 因为中国从1890年开始都有战争, 所以国家与人民都很穷, 能读完高中已经很了不起。

你爷爷读完高中后就变成了房子工程师, 他是我们那边唯一个能设计三层楼以上的人。你奶奶读完了小学(5年级), 就开始帮她的爸爸捕鱼挣钱，后来在她19岁时嫁给了你爷爷。然后有了你爸爸，就是我。再后来就有了你二叔，三叔和姑姐。

在1985年时我们一家移民到美国纽约，我们是你的姑婆(爷爷的姐姐)申请过来的。为什么要移民呢？那是因为美国的生活比我们在中国时好太多了。我是16岁时来美國的，在Seward Park High School重读9年和10年级，因为英文水平跟不上。那时候，我是一边读书一边打工，是很辛苦的，但是基本上很多像我这样年纪的人都是这样的。

读完高中后，我顺利进了大学，读电脑与经济。在读大学期间，有幸认识你的妈妈。读完大学，找到做电脑相关工作，做几年后，就和你妈结婚了，后来就生下了你和你弟弟。你的到来给了我们另一个生人目标，整家人都以你为宝贝。你漂亮，聪明，活泼.每个家族成员都喜欢你。

两年后，我们很幸运又生了一个非常英俊和聪明的男孩，你的弟弟Derek,你弟弟小时候很皮，可能这是男孩跟女孩的区别吧。在爷爷与奶奶的帮助下，你们很顺利地完成你们小学与中学。

因工作需要，我考了几个电脑网路工程师牌，受到公司重任，一路高升，一做就做了20年了。在同一家公司做了20年后，感觉是时候出来自己创业了，所以我三年前自己出来搞房地生意。

20年过去了，你和你弟弟也长大成年了，都完成了大学。我们很幸运也很骄傲的说：把你们培养成一个出色，自信，自重， 人品与道德都很好的人。现在，你们到了人生的另一个阶段，我和你妈都希望你们能好好地把握每一阶段,去创造你们自己的世界与未来。未来的路很长，我们必须保持上进心，希望你也能做到，学习是终生的，要记住。最后，谢谢你的妈妈，她是一个美丽，善良与勇敢的人，给我了这么优秀的孩子,她丰富了我的人生。

爸爸

June 25, 2021
The Growth of Our Family and You and Your Brother

Dear Daughter, Janette,

As per your request, today I will talk about our background, so you know where you came from. You will also know more about the differences in lifestyles and cultures of each generation.

Your mother and I are both from a small city named Taishan in southern China. It is a very famous and beautiful place. The first Chinese people to come to the United States came from Taishan. Regarding family members, we can start by talking about your grandfather's generation. I don't know much about the previous generations. Your grandfather has two brothers and two sisters. He was the youngest one. Your grandfather was born in a small town called Chonglou. The other brothers and sisters were all born in the countryside.

It is said that in the 1930s, because of disputes between the villages, their village was burned down, so they moved out of the small town. Your grandfather graduated from high school. It was not easy at that time, because China has had wars since 1890, so the country and people are very poor. It is already amazing to be able to finish high school.

Your grandpa became an architect after he finished high school. He is the only one on our side who can design more than three story homes. After your grandma finished elementary school (fifth grade), she began to help her father catch fish to earn money, and later married your grandfather when she was nineteen years old. Then, they had your dad, which is me. Later, they had your second uncle, third uncle, and aunt.

In 1985, our family immigrated to New York, and it was your aunt (grandfather's sister) who applied for us to come.

Why did we immigrate? That's because life in the United States is much better than when we were in China. I came to the United States when I was sixteen years old. At Seward Park High School, I got left back in the ninth and tenth grades because my English level could not keep up. At that time, I was working while studying, which was very hard, but basically, many people my age were also doing this.

After finishing high school, I successfully entered university, studying computer science and economics. During college, I had the honor of meeting your mother. After college, I found a computer-related job, and after a few years of working, I married your mother, and later gave birth to you and your brother. Your arrival has given us another purpose in life, and the whole family regards you as a treasure. You are beautiful, smart and lively. Every family member likes you a lot.

Two years later, we were lucky to have another very handsome and smart boy, your brother Derek, who was very naughty when he was a child. Maybe this is the difference between a boy and a girl. With the help of your grandpa and grandma, you both successfully completed your elementary and middle schools.

Due to work needs, I took a few computer network engineering licenses and received heavy work responsibilities. Once I started, I ended up staying for twenty years. After working in the same company for twenty years, I felt it was time to come out and start my own business, so I started my own real estate business three years ago.

Twenty years have passed, and you and your brother have grown up and have both completed college. We are very fortunate and proud to say we have cultivated you to be an outstanding, confident, self-respecting person with good character and morals. Now that you have reached another stage in your life, your mother and I hope you can seize each stage well to create your own world and future. The road ahead is very long. We must stay motivated and hope you can do the same. Learning is a lifelong process—remember this. Finally, thank you to your mother. She is a beautiful, kind, and brave person who gave me such an outstanding child. She has enriched my life.

Dad

Photo Album

"Oh, the pre-children good old days"
(Mom and Dad eating at a Chinese restaurant in 1996.)

“What a cute baby boy!” (One year old Janette with Grandma in the streets of Macau, China.)

“More Sprite please” (Janette eating dinner with Grandma and Grandpa at a Chinese restaurant.)

"Say onion rings in 3…2…1"
(Family picture on Derek's second birthday in 2001, not 1994.)

"Shoes in the house are okay for pictures."
(Dad with Janette and Derek in their Brooklyn home.)

“That’s for stealing my fruit roll-ups” (Janette is putting her younger brother, Derek, in an attempted chokehold.)

“Just kidding, I love you stupid” (Janette is cheesing with her younger brother, Derek.)

"Can we eat yet?"
(Family picture at yet another Chinese restaurant on New Year's Eve.)

"Is this the American or Canadian side?"
(Grandma and Grandpa at Niagara Falls)

"Coming home"
(First time visiting Dad's childhood home built by Grandpa in Taishan, China. Taken in August 2018.)

"Hurry up, I need to wrap the Zong Zi"
(After graduating amid a global pandemic in 2020, Janette takes her belated graduation photos in 2021 with Grandma.)

"The twenty-one ticks were worth it" (Janette hikes Wyanokie High Point in New Jersey with her dog, Montao.)

"Did you get heavier?" (Janette takes graduation pictures at Brooklyn Bridge Park in DUMBO with Rauful.) Photo Credit: Alejandro Quintero

Acknowledgments

It was May 6, 2020, and I woke up in the dark, dazed and confused, wondering if I had slept for only ten minutes or ten hours. Like many great ideas, the idea for this book came from a result of a late afternoon nap. When I first set out on this book journey, I didn't know what I was getting myself into. I knew that writing a book would take more than caffeine and hard work. Instead, the book you have in your hands is the collective effort of my tribe—people who have not only believed in the vision for this book, but also believed in me.

Now that I am almost on the other side, I can't help but feel immense gratitude as I sit here and write one of the final pieces for this book, ten months later. Gratitude, not only for you, my reader, for coming along with me for what is only the beginning of my life journey, but also, for myself, for the newfound strength to persevere even when every muscle fiber is saying "Fuck no." In fact, the word "gratitude" can't even fully encompass the feelings I have toward the opportunity to publish this legacy project.

The making of this book and the appreciation for the tribe that helped bring this idea from a mere idea to fruition can be summarized with this Chinese idiom, 刻骨铭心—something so unforgettable and etched in my memory that it will forever be carved into my bones and engraved into my heart—it's a bit melodramatic, but after reading this book, are you really surprised?

This is the section of the book where I reflect and thank those who carried me to the finish line of this book journey. While my name is on this book, all the credit goes to everyone on this page. Thank you all for allowing me to turn this unrealized bucket list goal into a reality.

Without the unconditional love and support from my family, this book would not exist. Thank you to my family, Ye Ye (Grandpa), whose cup was always half full; Ma Ma (Grandma), who made all the chicken soups that fed me and the soul; Dad, who taught me the value of hard work and instilled in me an entrepreneurial spirit; Mom, who is overflowing with kindness and radiating positivity; Derek, who is lucky to have an amazing big sister; and my dog, Montao, for being the "goodest" boy in the entire world.

I'd also like to thank my person, Rauful, who witnessed me crying over this book more than editing it. He believed in me even when he didn't want to read my rough manuscript because he didn't want to "ruin the surprise." Thank you for reminding me that while the path less taken is the most terrifying, it's also the most worthwhile and fulfilling. You remind me that the moment we decide we don't have to live a life that others have predestined for us is the moment that we set ourselves free.

To my editors, Julie Summer Keenan, Chelsea Friday, Morgan Rohde, Katie Sigler and Jordana Megonigal: Thank you for extinguishing my dumpster fire of a manuscript. Without your keen eyes and words of encouragement, revising this book would have been the plot for the next *Mission: Impossible* movie.

To everyone at the New Degree Press team: Eric Koester, Brian Bies, Haley Newlin, and Linda Berardelli, for all the ongoing support and guidance, thank you for providing the backbone for me to bring my memories and stories to life.

This book wouldn't have been possible without Gjorgji Pejkovski, Eldar Huseynov, Nikola Tikoski, Grzegorz Laszczyk, and Andrea Bojkovska for putting up with my endless creative pursuits and design layout ideas.

A thousand thank yous to Ariel Tsai, Victoria Cheng, Alison Hong Merill, Lilian Li, Ryka Aoki, Jay Antani, and Lillian Chen for being on the frontlines to willingly read early drafts of *Letters to Home.*

A big no thank you to Sophie Newman, Fanny Li, and Joanne Chen for always saying discouraging comments like "I'm proud of you" and "You got this" even when I didn't.

Special thanks to Ramya Kumar, your "Frankenstein" doodles resurrected my memories back into the present day.

On behalf of all my ABC readers, 非常感谢—A huge thank you to Sunny Sun for all your Chinese translation help.

I'm forever indebted to my author community, the 180 individuals who used parts of their pandemic stimulus check to back this book. Thank you.

Aaron-Patrick Empedrado
Afroza Ahmed
Agnes Tan
Alejandro Quintero
Aleksandra Serafin
Alexa Campanella
Alison Wang
Alyse Rodriguez
Amanda Kwong
Angel Chen
Angela Chi
Angus Ma
Anna Li

Anthony Liang
Ariel Tsai
Ashley Loh
Ashley Tan
Asia Le
Audrey Moore
Austin Peters
Bing Ying Hu
Candice Yan
Carol Kress
Caroline Zhu
Casey Lam
Cheryl Chen
Christine Ly
Christopher Broyles
Christopher Chiang
Christopher Zhou
Cindy Huang
Cindy Huang
Cindy Ng
Connie Zhu
Cynthia Vance
Daniella Zaytseva
Derek Murphy
Derek Wu
Elaine Lu
Ellie Yeo
Emilie Dang
Emily Hui
Emily Kwok
Emily Nee
Emily Zhang
Eric Koester
Erica Lo
Esther Saychaleune
Fanny Li
Farhan Naeem
Fiona Ng
Fleurenz Villar
Frankie Xu
Garmen X
Gilda McCrann
Hannah Chen
Herman Ng
Holly Lin
Hunter Chinese Flagship
Iman M
Iris Leung
Ivy Mei
Jane Lynn
Jesna Wilson
Jesse Chen
Jessi Liang
Jessica Au
Jessica Wu
Jessica Wong
Jessie Wong
Jimmy Serafin
Joanne Chen
Joanne Chen
Joyce Leung
Joyce Wu
Judy lam
Judy Xie

Justin Park
Kateryna Okhrimchuk
Katherine Mei
Katie Jiang
Katrina Lin
Kaylin Camidge
Kellie Chan
Kelly Chen
Kelly Zhu
Kelly/Kei Chan
Kenny Lim
Kevin Chan
Kevin Chiu
Kim & Betty Lee
Kiram Tung
Lillian Chen
Lily Taylor
Lucy Cheung
Lucy Zhang
Lynlia Tso
Lynn Liu
Matthew Ho
Matthew Travers
Maura Lima
Maxine Lui
Megan Andres
Meii Chiang
Melissa Chan
Melissa Lent
Michael Starmer
Michelle Chang
Michelle Chen
Michelle Liu
Michelle Zhao
Minci Liang
Mona Liu
Moorea Maguire
Nanako Chung
Nancy Brancati
Nancy Fung
Natalia Wiater
Nathaniel Shabatayev
Neevetha Nadarajah
Nina Chuang
Nozimakhon
Omonullaeva
Olivia Melvin
Olivia Palacios
Phyllis DiNardi
Quennie Huang
Rachel Lu
Ramya Kumar
Rauful Hossain
Rebecca Alisandratos
Rene Sanger
Roy Wagner
Ryan Sung
Sabrina Chan
Sabrina Ferrara
Sabrina Xu
Sadia Chowdhury
Salman Siraj
Sam Thirakoune
Samantha Mei

Samantha Yap
Samara Schuman
Sandy Lee
Sandy Wu
Sarah Chambers
Selina Dang
Serena Ma
Sharon Young
Shiqi Ning
Silvia Huang
Sontaey Jones
Soon-Hee Shimizu
Sophia Newman
Sophie Gray
Sophie Lo
Stacey Pang
Stephanie Weng
Stephen Fung
Sunny Sun
Susanna Cheung
Taylor Choi
Terri Chau
Tiffany Chen
Tiffany Li
Tingting Fang
Tommy Wu
Victor Hoang
Victoria Cheng
Vivian Ly
Wen Li Wang
Winnie Chen
Xiangmin Mo
Yea Lee Kim
Yoselin Ramirez
Yu Liang
Ziru Bolen
Zita Chau
Zoë Arnaut

Lastly, I'd like to thank my former self, for embracing the suck and doing the damn thing. Throughout the many times she wanted to pull the plug on this book, she persisted. She knew her fear of regret is greater than her fear of uncertainty and failure.

Appendix

A LETTER TO MY READERS

Brown, Brené. *Dare to Lead: Brave Work. Tough Conversations. Whole Hearts.* New York: Random House, 2018.

Kalanithi, Paul, and Abraham Verghese. *When Breath Becomes Air.* New York: Penguin Random House, 2016.

Obama, Michelle. *Becoming.* New York: Crown Publishing Group, 2018.

Wong, Ali. *Dear Girls: Intimate Tales, Untold Secrets & Advice for Living Your Best Life.* New York: Penguin Random House, 2019.

CHAPTER 1

Chapman, Gary D. *The 5 Love Languages.* Chicago: Northfield Publishing, 1992.

Islamic Council of Victoria. "What is Halal? A Guide for Non-Muslims." Accessed March 15th, 2021. *https://www.icv.org.au/about/about-islam-overview/what-is-halal-a-guide-for-non-muslims/.*

Specter, Michael. "Drool." *The New Yorker,* November 17, 2014. *https://www.newyorker.com/magazine/2014/11/24/drool.*

CHAPTER 3

Bancroft, Tony, and Barry Cook. *Mulan.* Film. Bay Lake, Florida: Walt Disney Pictures, 1998.

Chu, Jon. M. *Crazy Rich Asians.* Film. Burbank, California: Warner Bros. Pictures, 2018.

CHAPTER 6

Du Bois, W. E. B. (William Edward Burghardt). *The Souls of Black Folk; Essays and Sketches.* Chicago: A. G. McClurg, 1903. New York: Johnson Reprint Corp., 1968.

CHAPTER 7

Story, Tim. *Fantastic Four.* Film. New York City, New York: Marvel Enterprises, 2005.

Wong, Ali. *Dear Girls: Intimate Tales, Untold Secrets & Advice for Living Your Best Life.* New York: Penguin Random House, 2019.

CHAPTER 8

Levin, Brian. *Report to the Nation: Anti-Asian Prejudice & Hate Crime.* San Bernardino, CA: Center for the Study of Hate & Extremism CSUSB, 2021. *https://www.csusb.edu/sites/default/files/Report%20to%20the%20Nation%20-%20Anti-Asian%20Hate%202020%20Final%20Draft%20-%20As%20of%20Apr%2030%202021%206%20PM%20corrected.pdf*

Petri, Alexandra E. and Slotnik, Daniel E. "Attacks on Asian Americans in New York Stoke Fear, Anxiety and Anger."

New York Times, February 26th 2021. *https://www.nytimes.com/2021/02/26/nyregion/asian-hate-crimes-attacks-ny.html*

Science Encyclopedia. "Survival of the Fittest." Accessed May 8th, 2021. *https://science.jrank.org/pages/6637/Survival-Fittest.html.*

CHAPTER 9

Bo Ren (@Bosefina). Twitter post. Dec 1, 2017. 5:32 PM. *https://twitter.com/Bosefina/status/936724598632210433.*

CHAPTER 10

Katy Perry. "California Gurls." Track 3 on *Teenage Dream*. Capitol, 2010, compact disc.

Meyers, Nancy. *The Parent Trap*. Film. Bay Lake, Florida: Walt Disney Pictures, 1998.

CHAPTER 12

John Behring dir. *The 100*. Season 1, episode 9, "Unity Day." Aired May 14, 2014, on CW. *https://www.netflix.com/title/70283264.*

Kenan, Gil. *Monster House*. Film. Culver City, California: Columbia Pictures, 2006.

CHAPTER 13

Kalanithi, Paul, and Abraham Verghese. *When Breath Becomes Air.* New York: Penguin Random House, 2016.

CHAPTER 14

National Chicken Council. "Chickopedia: What Consumers Need to Know." Accessed February 4th, 2021. *https://www.nationalchickencouncil.org/about-the-industry/chickopedia/#one.*

EPILOGUE I

Six Flags. "King Da Ka." Accessed June 18th, 2021. *https://www.sixflags.com/greatadventure/attractions/kingda-ka*.